بسم الله الرحمن الرحيم

TO THE READER

In all the books by the author, faith-related issues are explained in the light of Qur'anic verses and people are invited to learn Allah's words and to live by them. All the subjects that concern Allah's verses are explained in such a way as to leave no room for doubt or question marks in the reader's mind. The sincere, plain and fluent style employed ensures that everyone of every age and from every social group can easily understand the books. This effective and lucid narrative makes it possible to read them in a single sitting. Even those who rigorously reject spirituality are influenced by the facts recounted in these books and cannot refute the truthfulness of their contents.

This book and all the other works of the author can be read individually or discussed in a group at a time of conversation. Those readers who are willing to profit from the books will find discussion very useful in the sense that they will be able to relate their own reflections and experiences to one another.

In addition, it will be a great service to the religion to contribute to the presentation and reading of these books, which are written solely for the good pleasure of Allah. All the books of the author are extremely convincing. For this reason, for those who want to communicate the religion to other people, one of the most effective methods is to encourage them to read these books.

It is hoped that the reader will take time to look through the review of other books on the final pages of this book, and appreciate the rich source of material on faith-related issues, which are very useful and a pleasure to read.

In these books, you will not find, as in some other books, the personal views of the author, explanations based on dubious sources, styles that are unobservant of the respect and reverence due to sacred subjects, nor hopeless, doubt-creating, and pessimistic accounts that create deviations in the heart.

The name of Jesus, peace be upon him, is 'Isa in Arabic, but since the intention in the author's writing of the book is to reach as many people, both Muslim and non-Muslim as possible, we have decided to retain the name which is most familiar to the greatest number of people today.

JESUS WILL RETURN

When the angels said, "Maryam, your Lord gives you good news of a Word from Him. His name is the Messiah, Jesus, son of Maryam of high esteem in the world and the Hereafter, and one of those brought near. (Surah Al 'Imran: 45)

HARUN YAHYA

December, 2006

Ta-Ha Publishers Ltd.
I Wynne Road London SW9 OBB

ABOUT THE AUTHOR

Now writing under the pen-name of HARUN YAHYA, he was born in Ankara in 1956. Having completed his primary and secondary education in Ankara, he studied arts at Istanbul's Mimar Sinan University and philosophy at Istanbul University. Since the 1980s, he has published many books on political, scientific, and faith-related issues. Harun Yahya is well-known as the author of important works disclosing the imposture of evolutionists, their invalid claims, and the dark liaisons between Darwinism and such ideologies as fascism and communism. Harun Yahya's works, translated into 57 different languages, constitute a collection of more than 45,000 pages with 30,000 illustrations.

His penname is a composite of the names *Harun* (Aaron) and *Yahya* (John), in memory of the two esteemed Prophets who fought against their peoples' lack of faith. The Prophet Muhammad's (saas) seal on his books' covers is symbolic and is linked to their contents. It represents the Qur'an (the final scripture) and the Prophet Muhammad (saas), last of the prophets. Under the guidance of the Qur'an and the Sunnah (teachings of the Prophet [saas]), the author makes it his purpose to disprove each fundamental tenet of irreligious ideologies and to have the 'last word', so as to completely silence the objections raised against religion. He uses the seal of the final Prophet (saas), who attained ultimate wisdom and moral perfection, as a sign of his intention to offer the last word.

All of Harun Yahya's works share one single goal: to convey the Qur'an's message, encourage readers to consider basic faith-related issues such as Allah's Existence and Unity and the Hereafter; and to expose irreligious systems' feeble foundations and perverted ideologies.

Harun Yahya enjoys a wide readership in many countries, from India to America, England to Indonesia, Poland to Bosnia, Spain to Brazil, Malaysia to Italy, France to Bulgaria and Russia. Some of his books are available in English, French, German, Spanish,

Italian, Portuguese, Urdu, Arabic, Albanian, Chinese, Swahili, Hausa, Dhivehi (spoken in Mauritius), Russian, Serbo-Croat (Bosnian), Polish, Malay, Uygur Turkish, Indonesian, Bengali, Danish and Swedish.

Greatly appreciated all around the world, these works have been instrumental in many people recovering faith in Allah and gaining deeper insight into their faith. His books' wisdom and sincerity, together with a distinct style that is easy to understand, directly affect anyone who reads them. Those who seriously consider these books can no longer advocate atheism or any other perverted ideology or materialistic philosophy, since these books are characterised by rapid effectiveness, definite results, and irrefutability. Even if they continue to do so, it will be only a sentimental insistence, since these books refute such ideologies from their very foundations. All contemporary movements of denial are now ideologically defeated, thanks to the books written by Harun Yahya.

This is no doubt a result of the Qur'an's wisdom and lucidity. The author modestly intends to serve as a means in humanity's search for Allah's right path. No material gain is sought in the publication of these works.

Those who encourage others to read these books, to open their minds and hearts and guide them to become more devoted servants of Allah, render an invaluable service.

Meanwhile, it would only be a waste of time and energy to propagate other books that create confusion in people's minds, lead them into ideological chaos, and that clearly have no strong and precise effects in removing the doubts in people's hearts, as also verified from previous experience. It is impossible for books devised to emphasise the author's literary power rather than the noble goal of saving people from loss of faith, to have such a great effect. Those who doubt this can readily see that the sole aim of Harun Yahya's books is to overcome disbelief and to disseminate the Qur'an's moral values. The success and impact of this service are manifested in the readers' conviction.

One point should be kept in mind: The main reason for the continuing cruelty, conflict, and other ordeals endured by the vast majority of people is the ideological prevalence of disbelief. This can be ended only with the ideological defeat of disbelief and by conveying the wonders of creation and Qur'anic morality so that people can live by it. Considering the state of the world today, leading into a downward spiral of violence, corruption and conflict, clearly this service must be provided speedily and effectively, or it may be too late.

In this effort, the books of Harun Yahya assume a leading role. By the will of Allah, these books will be a means through which people in the twentyfirst century will attain the peace, justice, and happiness promised in the Qur'an.

Published by:
Ta-Ha Publishers Ltd.
1 Wynne Road
London SW9 OBB

Website: http://www.taha.co.uk
E-mail: sales @ taha.co.uk

By Harun Yahya
Translated By: Mustapha Ahmad
Edited By: Abdassamad Clarke

A catalog record of this book is available from the British Library
ISBN 1 84200022 5

Printed and bound by:
FSF Matbaacilik in İstanbul
Address: Baglarici Mevkii Firuzkoy Caddesi No: 44
Avcilar - İstanbul / Turkiye
Phone: (+90 212) 690 8989

www.harunyahya.com

Abbreviations used:
as – (*'alayhi's-salam*):Peace be upon him (following a reference to the prophets or angels)
as – (*'alayha-salam*): Peace be upon her (following a reference to Maryam,
the Mother of Jesus (as))
saas – (*sallallahu alayhi wa sallam*): Peace and blessings be upon him
(following the name of the Prophet Muhammad)

All translations from the Qur'an are from *The Noble Qur'an: a New Rendering of its Meaning in English* by Hajj Abdalhaqq and Aisha Bewley, published by Bookwork, Norwich,
UK. 1420 CE/1999 AH.

CONTENTS

INTRODUCTION

*L*ike all the other prophets, Jesus ('Isa) (as) is a chosen slave of Allah whom Allah assigned to summon people to the true path. However, Allah has given Jesus (as) some attributes distinguishing him from other prophets, the most important one being that he was raised up to Allah and that he will come back to earth again.

Contrary to what most people believe, Jesus (as) was not crucified and killed nor did he die for any other reason. The Qur'an tells us that they did not kill him and they did not crucify him and that Allah raised him up to Him. Furthermore, the Qur'an acquaints us with some events from the life of Jesus (as) which have not yet happened. Thus, his second coming to earth is a prerequisite for these events to happen. There is no doubt that the events related in the Qur'an will certainly happen.

In addition we are told in a great many reliable hadiths[1] of the Prophet Muhammad (saas) that Jesus (as) is alive in the sight of Allah and will return to earth, and that when he does so he will rule with the Qur'an, be a means whereby the Christian world turns to Islam, and will, together with the Mahdi[2], make Islamic moral values prevail all over the world. Great Islamic scholars are in agreement that Jesus (as) did not die and will return to earth. Despite this, however, some people assume that Jesus (as) passed away some thousands of years ago and that thus it is unlikely that he will return. This is a misconception arising from lack of knowledge about the Qur'an and the hadith.

The Prophet Muhammad (saas) also told us that in the time when Jesus (as) will be sent back to earth, which is called 'the end of time', there will be a period in which the earth will attain unprecedented peace, justice and welfare.

The 'end times' refers to the period of time close to the end of the world. According to Islam, in this time, there will be the terrible trials of the *Dajjal* (Anti-Christ), many earthquakes and the emergence of Yajuj and Majuj (Gog and Magog) after which the ways of the Qur'an will prevail and people will extensively adhere to the values it teaches.

Evidence that Jesus (as) did not die, that he was raised to the presence of Allah and that he will return again will be examined in this book in the light of the Qur'anic verses, hadiths and Islamic scholars' interpretations. However, before proceeding, it would be beneficial to remind ourselves of some basic information directly related to this subject.

THE RELIGION WITH ALLAH IS ISLAM

*T*hroughout history, Allah has sent His messengers to many peoples. These messengers of Allah summoned mankind to the true path and communicated to them His ways. However today, some believe that the various messengers brought different religions to mankind. This is a misconception. The religions revealed by Allah to separate peoples in distinct periods were in fact one and the same. For instance, although the revelation given to Jesus (as) abolished some of the prohibitions of the previous revelation, there are in principle no huge differences between the religions revealed by Allah. What has been revealed to the former prophets, to Musa (Moses) (as), to Jesus (as) and to the last Prophet Muhammad (saas) are essentially the single true religion in Allah's sight. Verses of the Qur'an confirm this:

> Say, "We believe in Allah and what has been sent down
> to us and what was sent down to Ibrahim (Abraham),
> Isma'il (Ishmael) and Ishaq (Isaac) and Ya'qub (Jacob)
> and the Tribes, and what Musa (Moses) and 'Isa (Jesus)
> and all the Prophets were given by their Lord. We do
> not differentiate between any of them. We are Muslims
> submitted to Him. If anyone desires anything other

than Islam as a religion, it will not be accepted from
him, and in the Hereafter he will be among the losers."
(Surah Al 'Imran: 84-85)

These verses indicate that the right way revealed to man is
Islam and that all the prophets summoned their peoples to a
common way.

In another verse Allah ordains: "... I am pleased with Islam
as a religion *(deen)* for you!" (Surat al-Ma'ida: 3). Allah sent His
messengers to convey this religion, the one He is pleased with, to
their peoples and thus warn mankind. Each person, to whom
Allah's message is conveyed, and who is thus summoned to this
religion is held responsible for adhering to it.

However, some societies have accepted the message while
others have denied it. In some societies, on the other hand, the
right way has degenerated into perverted beliefs after the death
of their messenger. This is related in the Qur'an as follows:

The Religion with Allah is Islam. Those given the Book
only differed after knowledge had come to them, envy-
ing one another. As for those who reject Allah's Signs,
Allah is swift at reckoning. (Surah Al 'Imran: 19)

One of the societies that went astray after following the
right way for a while was a section of the Children of Israel *(Bani
Isra'il)*. As the Qur'an informs us, Allah sent many prophets to
the Children of Israel and informed them about the right way.
Yet, each time some of them revolted against a prophet or, after
the death of a prophet, they transformed the right way into a set
of perverted beliefs. Furthermore, from the Qur'an we know that
even when Musa (Moses) (as) was still alive, some among the
Children of Israel worshipped the golden calf during his short

absence (See Surah Ta Ha: 83-94). After the death of Musa (as), Allah sent many other prophets to the Children of Israel to warn them and the last of these prophets was Jesus (as).

Throughout his life, Jesus (as) called his people to live by the religion *(deen)* revealed by Allah and reminded them to be true slaves of Allah. He instructed them in the commandments of the *Injil* – the revelation granted to him, fragments of which may survive in parts of the Gospels. The *Injil* affirmed the commandments of the Tawrah – the revelation granted to Musa (as), some of which remains in the Torah and in the Old Testament – which had by then been corrupted. Criticising the improper teachings of the rabbis who were responsible for the degeneration of the true religion *(deen)*, Jesus (as) abolished the false rules that were invented by some rabbis themselves and through which they derived personal gain. He summoned the Children of Israel to the unity of Allah, to truthfulness, and to virtuous conduct. The Qur'an tells us:

> I come confirming the Tawrah I find already there, and to make lawful for you some of what was previously forbidden to you. I have brought you a sign from your Lord. So have fear of Allah and obey me. (Surah Al 'Imran: 50)

However, after Jesus (as) left the earth, some of his later followers started to corrupt the revelation. Under the influence of some pagan ideas from the Greeks, they developed a perverted belief in the 'Trinity' (the Father, the Son and the Holy Ghost) (Surely Allah is beyond that). Under the name of Christianity, they adhered to a totally different religion. Although the Christianity of today contains some beliefs and practices belonging to the true faith, the religion revealed to Jesus (as) has been corrupted by certain individuals who came after him. Many years after the first coming of Jesus (as), unidentified people authored the books of what we know today as the New Testament, and they wrote them in Greek whereas the language of Jesus (as) and his disciples was Aramaic, a language close to Arabic. In succeeding ages, historians compiled these writings. Consequently, Christianity today has lost much of Jesus' (as) original teaching.

After Jesus (as), Allah sent another messenger from a different tribe in order that through him He could reveal and restore the original religion to the world, and He endowed him with a noble book. This messenger was the Prophet Muhammad (saas) and the book is the Qur'an, the only unaltered Divine revelation.

The Qur'an addresses all mankind and is relevant for all times. All people from all ages will be held responsible for adhering to this book, if they have been exposed to the message of Islam. They will be judged according to the Qur'an on the Day of Judgement. In this day and age especially, all the nations of the world are, in a sense, united and have almost become like a single tribe, thanks to technological breakthroughs. One academic referred to the world today as 'the global village'. Therefore, there are few people in the world today who can be unaware of the existence of the Qur'an and who are uninformed about Islam. Despite this, only a certain part of people has faith in the Qur'an.

It is glad tidings implied in the Qur'an and reported in detail in the hadith that Jesus (as) will come back to earth and summon people to the right way so that the contradictory state of affairs that present-day Christians find themselves in will be resolved. As will be dealt with in succeeding chapters of this book, Jesus (as) was raised up to the presence of Allah and has not yet died a physical death. After a while, he will return and, as related in the hadith, make Islam prevail in the world together with the Mahdi. To the best of their abilities, both the Christian and the Muslim worlds are preparing to meet this blessed visitor and to merit his superior morality.

PEOPLE IN TROUBLE BEG FOR A SAVIOUR

What reason could you have for not fighting in the Way of Allah – for those men, women and children who are oppressed and say, "Our Lord, take us out of this city whose inhabitants are wrongdoers! Give us a protector from You! Give us a helper from You!"? (Surat an-Nisa: 75)

We learn from the Qur'an that very often social and moral corruption was prevalent in a nation before a messenger was sent to that society. Once a messenger came to that society, those following him attained a blissful, peaceful and bountiful life even in the midst of their honourable struggle for the good pleasure of Allah. After this blessed period, however, some people drifted away from their spiritual values, revolted and ultimately tended almost to disbelief. In some cases, they worshipped gods other than Allah and thus were unjust to their own selves.

In the Qur'an, Allah relates the loyalty, sincerity and fear the messengers felt for Allah and then informs us of how some generations coming after them lost their faith completely. They drifted because of their whims and desires and became deprived of all their values. The Qur'an tells us about these people in the following words:

Those are some of the Prophets Allah has blessed, from the descendants of Adam and from those We carried with Nuh (Noah), and from the descendants of Ibrahim (Abraham) and Isra'il (Israel) and from those We guided and chose. When the signs of the All-Merciful were recited to them, they fell on their faces, weeping in prostration. An evil generation succeeded them who neglected the prayers and followed their appetites. They will plunge into the Valley of Evil. (Surah Maryam: 58-59)

Those people who neglected their divine responsibilities suffered Allah's wrath expressed through various disasters. Allah withdrew His favour from these people. In accordance with the verse **"But if anyone turns away from My reminder, his life will be a dark and narrow one..."** (Surah Ta Ha: 124), they suffered from different afflictions such as scarcity and social and economic problems arising from their moral degeneration and political instability.

Under irreligious systems, those people who were insolent towards the divine revelation were exposed to various pressures and injustices. The period of Pharaoh *(Fir'awn)* is a typical example recounted in the Qur'an. Exulting in his affluence, Pharaoh led an extravagant life and his people suffered under his tyranny. This situation is explained in the Qur'an:

Pharaoh exalted himself arrogantly in the land and divided its people into camps, oppressing one group of

**them by slaughtering their sons and letting their
women live. He was one of the corrupters. (Surat al-
Qasas: 4)**

Under such circumstances where people suffer economic
and social problems under the tyranny of unjust leaders, the
need for a saviour is profoundly felt. This is the person who
removes the unfavourable aspects of the system caused by the
disbelief *(kufr)* of the ruler and his people and brings the peace,
justice and security which come along with obedience to Allah
and His Messenger.

After the Prophet Musa (Moses) (as), the Children of Israel
also faced the same difficulties under the rule of tyrants. They
were driven from their homes and lands and suffered intensely.
Realising that neither the idols they worshipped, nor their pos-
sessions, nor ancestors would save them from such undesirable
circumstances, they asked for a king from Allah; a saviour who
would save them from this cruel system.

"You Will Not Find Any Changing in the Pattern of Allah"

From the stories related in the Qur'an, we understand that
almost the same fate befell each of the past civilisations that
revolted against their messengers. The circumstances under
which people led their lives, the sending of messengers to warn
them and destruction of some of them all follow the same pattern.

Modern societies also undergo rapid corruption and degeneration. Poverty, misery and disorder throw the lives of people
into complete disarray and make them wish for a peaceful life
where virtue prevails. Apparently, justice can prevail only if the

values of the Qur'an become predominant among people. Only people having real values can bring solutions to all the troubles that people experience today. Indeed, Allah sent prophets and messengers to the earlier generations who experienced similar social depressions, and He sometimes granted amazing blessings to those who followed the messengers. This is related in the following verse:

If only the people of the cities had had faith and feared, We would have opened up to them blessings from heaven and earth. But they denied the truth so We seized them for what they earned. (Surat al-A'raf: 96)

This verse, as well as many others confirming it, reveals that the one and only way to attain bliss and peace is adherence to Islam. This principle will apply to coming generations as it did to previous ones. In places bereft of Islam, injustice, insecurity and instability prevail. This is the law of Allah. That there exists no change in the law of Allah is stated in the Qur'an:

... But then when a warner did come to them, it only increased their aversion, shown by their arrogance in the land and evil plotting. But evil plotting envelopes only those who do it. Do they expect anything but the pattern of previous peoples? <u>You will not find any changing in the pattern of Allah. You will not find any alteration in the pattern of Allah.</u> (Surah Fatir: 42-43)

Living Islam According to the Qur'an

As mentioned in the previous section, the Qur'an informs us that Allah sends prophets and messengers to communities for their deliverance from disbelief and injustice. This prophet or messenger leads his people to believe (have *iman*) in Allah without ascribing partners to Him, and to fear Him. If the community persists in denial, he warns them of Allah's wrath. Allah tells us in the Qur'an that He destroys no tribe before this warning is delivered:

We have never destroyed a city without giving it prior warning as a reminder. We were never unjust. (Surat ash-Shu'ara: 208-209)

In the age in which we live, one observes degeneration, both physical and spiritual, in society at large accompanied by economic and political instability. Huge gaps exist between rich and poor, and social corruption is steadily escalating. All these point to significant developments that will take place in the near future. After and even during such dark periods, Allah always shows the way to salvation to those who earnestly desire it. In this way, the religion of Allah will certainly prevail over the entire world and the true religion will supersede all pagan religions. To His true believers *(muminun)*, Allah gives good tidings of this:

But Allah refuses to do other than perfect His Light, even though the unbelievers detest it. It is He who sent His Messenger with guidance and the Religion of Truth to exalt it over every other religion, even though those who associate partners with Allah (mushrikun) detest it. (Surat at-Tawba: 32-33)

In Surat an-Nur, Allah informs his true believers who engage in "right actions" without associating partners with Him and who purely seek His good pleasure, that they will attain power, as preceding believers always did:

Allah has promised those of you who believe and do

right actions that He will make them successors in the land as He made those before them successors, and firmly establish for them their religion with which He is pleased and give them, in place of their fear, security. "They worship Me, not associating anything with Me." Any who disbelieve after that, such people are deviators. (Surat an-Nur: 55)

In the above verse, we learn that the criterion for the spread of Islam is the existence of believers who are purely slaves of Allah without ascribing partners to Him and who engage in good deeds in His way.

We have seen that in every age, Allah has answered the call of His slaves who desperately needed His help. This also holds true for this age and for the future. As was the case with earlier ages, in our time, too, Allah will save people from the injustice of the system of disbelief and present them with the beauty of Islam.

In particular, the deliverance of the Islamic world from the troubles that beset it, as revealed in the hadith, is close at hand. Surely, as in every age, today people hope that a saviour will appear. This saviour, that will take mankind from 'darkness to the light,' is the religion of Islam. Jesus (as) and the Mahdi, who will be the means whereby people will live by these superior values, will defeat intellectually all the systems that deny Allah, and they will render corrupted ideologies invalid.

Allah promises His help to His slaves who sincerely turn to Him and have deep fear of Him:

Those who were expelled from their homes without any right merely for saying, "Our Lord is Allah". If Allah had not driven some people back by means of others, monasteries, churches, synagogues and mosques, where Allah's name is mentioned much, would have been pulled down and destroyed. <u>Allah will certainly help those who help Him</u> – Allah is all-Strong, Almighty, those who, if We establish them firmly on the earth, will establish prayer and pay the poor-due, and command what is right and forbid what is wrong. The end result of all affairs is with Allah. (Surat al-Hajj: 40-41)

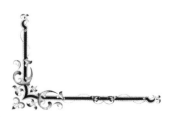

JESUS (AS),
SON OF MARYAM (AS),
IN THE QUR'AN

*T*his section looks at the details regarding the second coming of Jesus (as) as found in the most reliable sources. The first of these sources is most certainly the Qur'an, the unaltered Speech of Allah, as expressed in the Qur'an, **"No one can change His words"** (Surat al-An'am 115); and the second is the Sunnah of the Last Messenger of Allah, Muhammad (saas). The Qur'an provides detailed information about many stages of Jesus' (as) life including his birth, his being raised to the presence of Allah, his second coming and his death.

Jesus (as), who lived some two thousand years ago, is a blessed messenger of Allah. He is held in high esteem both in this world and the Hereafter, as the Qur'an informs us. The true religion revealed to him still remains today, albeit in name only. That is because the original teaching communicated by Jesus (as) has been distorted. The book Allah revealed to Jesus (as), too, is distorted. Christian sources have undergone various alterations and perversions. Consequently today, it is unlikely that we can obtain true knowledge regarding Jesus (as) from Christian sources.

The only sources from which we can gain accurate knowledge about Jesus (as) are the Qur'an, the book Allah assures He will keep unchanged until the Day of Judgement, and the Sunnah of His Messenger Muhammad (saas). In the Qur'an, Allah gives an account of the birth and life of Jesus (as), some incidents he met in his life, the people surrounding him and many other subjects related to him. Furthermore, the Qur'anic verses also inform us about the life of Maryam (as) before she gave birth to Jesus (as), how she conceived in a miraculous way and the reactions of the people surrounding her to this incident. Moreover, some verses of the Qur'an imply that Jesus (as) will come to earth for a second time in the end times. This section presents some of this Qur'anic information.

The Birth of Maryam (as) and the Way She Was Raised

Maryam (as), who was chosen to give birth to Jesus (as), was born at a time of social disorder when the Children of Israel placed all their hopes on a Messiah's coming. Allah specially chose Maryam (as) for this blessed duty and brought her up accordingly. Maryam (as) came from a noble family, the family of 'Imran. Allah chose this family over all people.

The members of the family of 'Imran were known to be people having great faith in Allah. They turned to Him while doing all their deeds and meticulously observed His limits. When 'Imran's wife learned that she was expecting a child, she turned to her Creator and prayed, and she devoted what was in her womb to the service of Allah. Allah gives an account of this in the Qur'an:

Remember when the wife of 'Imran said, "My Lord, I

have pledged to You what is in my womb, devoting it to
Your service. Please accept my prayer. You are the All-
Hearing, the All-Knowing." When she gave birth, she
said, "My Lord! I have given birth to a girl" – and Allah
knew very well what she had given birth to, male and
female are not the same – "and I have named her
Maryam and placed her and her children in Your safekeeping from the accursed shaytan." (Surah Al 'Imran:
35-36)

When Maryam (as) was born, Imran's wife sought only the
good pleasure of Allah. She turned to Allah and placed Maryam
(as) and her children in His safekeeping from the accursed shaytan. In return for her sincerity and prayer, Allah gave Maryam
(as) noble virtues. In the Qur'an, Allah explains how Maryam
(as) was brought up under His protection and meticulous care.
**"Her Lord accepted her with approval and made her grow in
health and beauty."** (Surah Al 'Imran: 37). Zakariyya (Zachariah)
(as) became Maryam's (as) guardian and during the time she
spent with him, he realised that she was favoured with exceptional qualities. Moreover, Allah showed her many favours:

... Every time Zakariyya (Zachariah) visited her in the
Upper Room, he found food with her. He said,
"Maryam, how did you come by this?" She said, "It is
from Allah. Allah provides for whomever He wills
without any reckoning." (Surah Al 'Imran: 37)

Just as Allah chose the family of 'Imran, He also chose
Maryam (as), a member of 'Imran's family, and provided her
with an exceptional upbringing. Allah purified Maryam (as) and
chose her over all other women. This attribute of hers is stated in
the Qur'an:

And when the angels said, "Maryam, Allah has chosen
you and purified you. He has chosen you over all other
women. Maryam, obey your Lord and prostrate and
bow with those who bow." (Surah Al 'Imran: 42-43)

In the community in which she lived, Maryam (as) became
known for the loyalty and sincerity she showed to Allah. She is
especially distinguished as a woman "who guarded her chastity".
In Surat at-Tahrim, we find an account of this:

Maryam, the daughter of 'Imran, who guarded her
chastity – We breathed Our Spirit into her and she confirmed the Words of her Lord and His Book and was
one of the obedient. (Surat at-Tahrim: 12)

Jesus (as) Was Born Without a Father

One of the greatest miracles Allah manifested on Jesus (as)
is the manner in which Maryam (as) conceived. The Qur'an gives
a great many details on this subject. The way that Jibril (Gabriel)
(as) appeared to her is described in these terms in Surah
Maryam:

Mention Maryam in the Book, how she withdrew from
her people to an eastern place, and veiled herself from
them. Then We sent Our Spirit to her and it took on for
her the form of a well-made man. (Surah Maryam: 16-
17)

As we are informed in the verses above, in one of the phas-
es of her life, Maryam (as) withdrew from her people to an eastern place and spent some part of her life there. At this time, Jibril
(as) appeared to her as a normal human being. Another important matter stressed in the verses is Maryam's (as) modest behav-

iour and strong fear of Allah. The first words she spoke when seeing Jibril (as) were:

"I seek refuge from you with the All-Merciful if you have taqwa." (Surah Maryam: 18)

Yet, Jibril (as) introduced himself and explained that he was a messenger sent by Allah to give her glad tidings. The verses report Jibril's (as) reply as being:

"I am only your Lord's messenger so that He can give you a pure boy." (Surah Maryam: 19)

When the angels said, "Maryam, your Lord gives you good news of a Word from Him. His name is the Messiah, 'Isa, son of Maryam of high esteem in the world and the hereafter, and one of those brought near." (Surah Al 'Imran: 45)

Upon hearing these glad tidings, Maryam (as) raised the question of how she could have a son when no man had ever touched her:

She said, "How can I have a boy when no one has touched me and I am not an unchaste woman?" He said, "It will be so! Your Lord says, 'That is easy for Me. It is so that We can make him a Sign for mankind and a mercy from Us.' It is a matter already decreed." So she conceived him and withdrew with him to a distant place. (Surah Maryam: 20-22)

She said, "My Lord! How can I have a son when no one has ever touched me?" He said, "It will be so." Allah creates whatever He wills. When He decides on something, He just says to it, 'Be!' and it is." (Surah Al 'Imran: 47)

As can be seen from the above verses, Jibril (as) gave Maryam (as) the glad tidings that she was with child and told her **"Allah just says to it, 'Be!' and it is."** Maryam (as) had never been touched by a man. In other words, Jesus (as) did not come into the world in the normal way in which children are created. This is just one of the miracles that Jesus (as) experienced during his life and will experience when he returns to earth for a second time, as a blessing of Allah.

During the time Maryam (as) remained in the "distant place", Allah supported her both physically and materially. She was totally under His protection and care during her pregnancy. Allah especially took care of all her needs. Meanwhile, by making her settle in a secluded place, Allah prevented all the harm that people devoid of understanding of this miracle were likely to do her.

Jesus (as) is a "Word of Allah"

In the Qur'an Allah draws our attention to the fact that, from his birth to death, Jesus (as) was very different from all other men on earth, as He willed so. The Qur'an confirms his virgin birth, a type of creation with which we are not familiar. Before Jesus (as) was born, Allah informed his mother about many of Jesus' (as) attributes including the fact that he was sent as a Messiah to the Children of Israel. He was also declared "a Word" from Allah:

> ... The Messiah, 'Isa, son of Maryam, was only the Messenger of Allah and His Word, which He cast into Maryam, and a Spirit from Him... (Surat an-Nisa: 171)

> When the angels said, "Maryam, your Lord gives you good news of a Word from Him. His name is the Messi-

ah, 'Isa, son of Maryam of high esteem in the world and the Hereafter, and one of those brought near. (Surah Al 'Imran: 45)

Allah gave him his name before his birth, as He did with Yahya (John) (as). Allah gave him the name the Messiah, 'Isa, the son of Maryam. This is one of the most explicit indications that Jesus (as) was created differently from other people.

Indeed, just like his birth, the miracles he displayed throughout his life with Allah's grace, and the way he was raised up to the presence of Allah are signs of his difference from other people.

Birth of Jesus (as)

As is well known, birth is a very difficult process demanding much care. Delivering a baby without the assistance of an experienced person and due medical care is difficult. However, Maryam (as), all alone, succeeded in delivering a baby, thanks to her loyalty to Allah and the trust she put in Him.

While feeling severe labour pains, Allah inspired Maryam (as) and instructed her in each step. In this way, she delivered her baby effortlessly and in the best circumstances. This was a great favour shown to Maryam (as):

The pains of labour drove her to the trunk of a date palm. She said, "Oh if only I had died and was something discarded and forgotten!"

A voice called out to her from under her, "Do not grieve! Your Lord has placed a small stream at your feet. Shake the trunk of the palm towards you and fresh, ripe dates will drop down onto you.

Eat and drink and delight your eyes. If you should see anyone at all, just say, 'I have made a vow of abstinence to the All-Merciful and today I will not speak to any human being.'" (Surah Maryam: 23-26)

Jesus (as) Spoke While Still in the Cradle

And she (Maryam) who guarded her chastity. We breathed in her some of Our Spirit and made her and her son a Sign for all the worlds. (Surat al-Anbiya: 91)

The birth of Jesus (as), which was an unusual event for people, was a test both for Maryam (as) and her people. In reality, the way Jesus (as) was born was a miracle Allah employed to summon people to true faith and one of the most explicit evidences of the existence of Allah. Yet, her people failed to grasp it and were suspicious. As mentioned in the Qur'an:

She brought him to her people, carrying him. They said, "Maryam! You have done an unthinkable thing! Sister of Harun (Aaron), your father was not an evil man nor was your mother an unchaste woman!" (Surah Maryam: 27-28)

As explained in the verses above, upon Maryam's (as) return from the distant place with Jesus (as), her people did not let her explain. They simply slandered Maryam (as) in an ugly manner. However, those who spread these slanders about Maryam (as) knew her almost from the day she was born and were aware of her purity and piety (taqwa), like the other members of the family of 'Imran.

Surely, these false accusations were a test for Maryam (as). It was apparent that a person, so pure and pious, would not overstep Allah's limits. From the time Maryam (as) was born, Allah always helped her and turned everything she did to good. Maryam (as), in return, knew that every incident happens by the Will of Allah and only Allah could prove the groundless nature of these slanders.

Indeed, Allah provided comfort to Maryam (as) and inspired her to remain quiet. Allah instructed her not to speak with her people but to point to Jesus (as), if they ever approached her and attempted to make accusations. In this way, Maryam (as) avoided any trouble such a discussion was likely to create. The one who would provide the most accurate answers to the people was Jesus (as). When Allah gave the good tidings of the birth of Jesus (as) to Maryam (as), He also informed her that he would speak clearly while he was still in his cradle:

> **He will speak to people in the cradle, and also when fully grown, and will be one of the righteous. (Surah Al 'Imran: 46)**

Thus Allah made things easier for Maryam (as) and provided the true explanation to the people through the words of Jesus (as). With such a miracle, the disbelief of the people surrounding Maryam (as) simply failed. We are informed in the Qur'an:

> **She pointed towards him. They said, "How can a baby in the cradle speak?" He said, "I am the slave of Allah. He has given me the Book and made me a Prophet. He has made me blessed wherever I am and directed me to do prayer and pay poor-due as long as I live, and to show devotion to my mother. He has not made me insolent or arrogant. Peace be upon me the day I was born, and the day I die and the day I am raised up again alive." (Surah Maryam: 29-33)**

No doubt, a baby speaking fluently in his cradle is a great miracle. The people of Maryam (as) were astonished on hearing these words of wisdom from a baby and this occasion proved to them that his birth was a miracle. All these miraculous incidents showed that the blessed baby in the cradle was a messenger of Allah.

This was Allah's mercy on Maryam (as) because of the trust she placed in Him. By means of such an astounding miracle, she responded to the slanders against her without having to say a word. Yet, Allah informs us that a grievous disaster awaited those who did not dismiss their bad thoughts about Maryam (as) despite this miracle:

> **And on account of their disbelief and their utterance of a monstrous slander against Maryam. (Surat an-Nisa: 156)**

Miracles of Jesus (as)

Jesus (as) performed many other miracles, by the permission of Allah, other than his virgin birth and his declaration of his prophethood as a new born child in the cradle. In fact, these two miracles are proof that Allah has chosen him. After all, only a miracle could make a new-born child speak so rationally and with faith:

> **Remember when Allah said: "'Isa, son of Maryam, remember My blessing to You and to your mother when I reinforced you with the Purest Spirit so that you could speak to people in the cradle and when you were fully grown; and when I taught you the Book and Wisdom..." (Surat al-Ma'ida: 110)**

In the Qur'an, the miracles of Jesus (as) are related thus:

... As a Messenger to the tribe of Israel, saying: "I have brought you a Sign from your Lord. I will create the shape of a bird out of a clay for you and then breathe into it and it will be a bird by Allah's permission. I will heal the blind and the leper, and bring the dead to life, by Allah's permission. I will tell you what you eat and what you store up in your homes. There is a Sign for you in that if you are believers. (Surah Al 'Imran: 49)

Despite all the miracles related so far, some people arrogantly rejected the miracles of Jesus (as) and said they were all magic.

Jesus (as) Communicated the Message, and Some of the Difficulties He Faced

At the time Jesus (as) was sent, the people of Israel were in complete turmoil, both in the political and the economic sense. On one hand, there were the cruel conditions inflicted on the public and, on the other, dissenting beliefs and sects made life difficult. Under such conditions, people desperately needed a way out.

The messenger that was to relieve this society of its difficulties was Jesus (as). By the will of Allah, Jesus (as) spoke when he was still in the cradle and thus indicated to people that the Messiah they expected had arrived. Some of the people realised that Jesus (as) was a messenger who had been sent, and believed in him.

Yet, there were also some people who avoided accepting Jesus (as). Supporters of the system of disbelief of his time, especially, considered him merely a threat to their irreligious system. That is why they made plans to prevent him as soon as they heard about him. To their dismay, however, their plans were doomed to failure from the beginning. Still, this did not stop them trying to realise their aim.

Nevertheless, those who reacted against him were not limited to disbelievers. During that period, for various reasons, a majority of the rabbis took sides against Jesus (as) asserting that he was abolishing their religion, and of course by that they became disbelievers because of their opposition to a Messenger of Allah. What Jesus (as) did, in reality, was only to summon people to the original way, and eliminate the false rules introduced into Judaism by some rabbis themselves. Some of the people of Israel distorted their religion by prohibiting what was allowed by the original revelation and allowing what was prohibited by it. In this way, they changed the true way revealed by Allah. Following this, Allah sent Jesus (as) to purify the true religion of all the innovations incorporated into it at a later stage. Jesus (as) called his people to the *Injil*, which confirmed the original *Tawrah* revealed to Musa (Moses) (as), as stated in the Qur'an:

> **"I come confirming the Tawrah I find already there, and to make lawful for you some of what was previously forbidden to you. So have fear of Allah and obey me." (Surah Al 'Imran: 50)**

In another verse Allah informs us that the *Injil* revealed to Jesus (as) was a guide to the true path for the believers to help them discern between good and evil. It was also a book that confirmed the *Tawrah*:

> **And we sent 'Isa son of Maryam following in their footsteps, confirming the Tawrah that came before him. We gave him the Injil containing guidance and light, confirming the Tawrah that came before it, and as guidance**

and admonition for those who have fear." (Surat al-Ma'ida: 46)

Some among the Children of Israel doubted what Jesus (as) had brought, but Jesus (as) summoned people to devotion to Allah, renunciation of the luxuries of this world, sincerity, brotherhood and honesty. He told them to avoid false beliefs and practices. In the Qur'an, Allah gives an account of how Jesus (as) communicated the commands of Allah:

And when 'Isa came with the Clear Signs, he said, "I have come to you with Wisdom and to clarify for you some of the things about which you have differed. Therefore have taqwa of (heed) Allah and obey me. Allah is my Lord and your Lord so worship Him. This is a straight path." The various factions among them differed. Woe then to those who did wrong on account of the punishment of a painful Day! (Surat az-Zukhruf: 63-65)

The sincerity and wise communication of Jesus (as) attracted people's attention. The number of his adherents steadily increased.

The Jews Claim They Killed Jesus' (as)

It is alleged that the Romans crucified Jesus (as). As the allegation goes, the Romans and some Jewish rabbis arrested Jesus (as) and crucified him. Indeed, the Christian world embraces the belief that Jesus (as) died but then came back to life again and ascended to heaven. However, the Qur'an tells us that this is not true, and that Jesus (as) neither died nor was killed:

And (on account of) their saying, "We killed (qatalna)

the Messiah, 'Isa son of Maryam, Messenger of Allah."
They did not kill *(wa ma qataloohu)* him and they did
not crucify *(wa ma salaboohu)* him but it was made to
seem so *(shubbiha)* to them. Those who argue about
him are in doubt about it. They have no real knowledge
of it, just conjecture. But they certainly did not kill (wa
ma qataloohu) him. (Surat an-Nisa': 157)

The Qur'an continues by stating that Jesus (as) was raised to
Allah:

Allah raised him up to Himself *(rafa'ahu)*. Allah is
Almighty, All-Wise. (Surat an-Nisa': 158)

The Qur'an states the facts very clearly: the attempts of the
Romans, provoked by some of the Jews to kill Jesus (as), proved
unsuccessful. The expression quoted from the above verse "...
but it was made to seem so to them" explains the real nature of
this event. Jesus (as) was not killed but he was raised up to
Allah's presence. Furthermore, Allah reveals that those making
this claim know nothing about the truth.

How Are Prophets' Deaths Recounted in the Qur'an?

Examination of the stories in the Qur'an that mention how
prophets died, and the verses that describe the ascension of Jesus
(as), reveal an important fact. In this section we shall examine the
meaning of the Arabic words used in the story of Jesus (as) as
well as those used to describe the deaths of other prophets, and
will see how they are used in the verses.

As we shall be seeing in greater detail later, a number of
words are used in the Qur'an to describe the deaths of prophets,

such as *qataloohu* (to kill), *maata* (to die), *halaka* (to perish) and *salaboohu* (they crucified him). However, it is clearly stated in the Qur'an that, "They did not kill him *(wa ma qataloohu)* and did not crucify him *(wa ma salaboohu)*", meaning Jesus (as) was not killed in any way. It is emphasised that, in fact, someone who resembled Jesus (as) was put forward and that Jesus (as) was raised to the presence of Allah.

In Surah Al 'Imran, we are informed that Allah took Jesus (as) back and He raised him up to Him.

When Allah said, "'Isa, I will take you back *(mutawaffeeka)* and raise you up *(wa rafi'uka)* to Me and purify you of those who are disbelievers. And I will place the people who follow you above those who are disbelievers until the Day of Rising..." (Surah Al 'Imran: 55)

The following are the ways in which the words referring to death in the Qur'an have been used.

1. *TAWAFFA*: TO CAUSE TO DIE, TO TAKE IN SLEEP OR TO TAKE BACK

The word *tawaffa* as used in this verse has other meanings than simply 'death' in English. A study of the Arabic equivalents of the words in the verses reveals that Jesus (as) did not die in the accepted sense. This is how his being taken back to Allah is described in Surat al-Ma'ida:

I said to them nothing but what You ordered me to say: "Worship Allah, my Lord and your Lord." I was a witness against them as long as I remained among them, but when You took me back to You *(tawaffa)*, You were the One watching over them. You are Witness of all things. (Surat al-Ma'ida: 117)

Surah Al 'Imran states:

When Allah said, "'Isa, I will take you back *(mutawaf-feeka)* **and raise you up** *(wa rafi'uka)* **to Me and purify you of those who are disbelievers. And I will place the people who follow you above those who are disbelievers until the Day of Rising..." (Surah Al 'Imran: 55)**

This verse informs the believers that Allah will "take back" Jesus (as), protect him from the unbelievers, and raise him to His presence. Many great Islamic scholars and commentators have interpreted this verse to mean that Jesus (as) did not die.

In Arabic the word that is translated in some translations of these verses as "You have caused me to die" is *tawaffa* and comes from the root wafa – to fulfil. In fact, in Arabic commentaries it is not used in the sense of death. The commentary of Imam al-Qurtubi is one example of this; he used the expression "the taking away of the selves" for the word in question. From the Qur'an again, we understand that "taking the self back" does not necessarily mean death. For instance in a verse in which the word *tawaffa* is used, it is not the death of a human being that is meant but "taking back his self in his sleep":

It is He Who <u>takes you back to Himself</u> *(yatawaffakum)* **at night, while knowing the things you perpetrate by day, and then** <u>wakes you up again, so that a specified term may be fulfilled</u>**... (Surat al-An'am: 60)**

The word used for "take back" in this verse is the same as the one used in Surah Al 'Imran 55. In other words, in the verse above, the word *tawaffa* is used and it is obvious that one does not die in one's sleep. Therefore, what is meant here is, again, "taking the self back."

The same word is used again in the verse below:

Allah takes back people's selves *(yatawaffa)* when their death *(mawtiha)* arrives and those who have not yet died, while they are asleep *(lam tamut)*. He keeps hold of those whose death (mawt) has been decreed and sends the others back for a specified term... (Surat az-Zumar: 42)

As these verses suggest, Allah takes back the self of the one who is asleep, yet He sends back the selves of those whose deaths have not yet been decreed. In this context, in one's sleep one does not die, in the sense in which we perceive death. Only for a temporary period, the self leaves the body and remains in another dimension. Upon waking up, the self returns to the body.

Another instance in which sleep is regarded as a kind of death, but which does not refer to biological death, is the following du'a, which the Prophet Muhammad (saas) often used to recite when he woke up: "All praise is for Allah, Who has made us alive after He made us die [sleep]. *(Al-hamdu li Allah illadhi ahyana ba'da maa amatana; wa ilayhi al-nushoo)*" (Narrated by Abu Hudhayfa; Sahih Bukhari).[3] No doubt, he used these wise words not to refer to biological death when one is asleep, but rather to a sleeping person's soul being "taken." Ibn Kathir, the famous Islamic scholar and commentator, used this hadith, along with many other proofs in his commentary on Surah Al 'Imran, to explain that *tawaffa* refers to sleep. In addition, he indicated the word's meaning in other verses where it appears. He then gave his opinion using a hadith handed down by Ibn Abi Hatim:

Ibn Abi Hatim says that: "My father told us ... from Hassan that the meaning of the verse 'I will take you back...' is this: Here it means that 'I shall kill you with the death of sleep; in other words, I shall cause you to sleep.' So Allah raised Jesus (as) to the heavens while he was asleep ... As an incontrovertible truth, Allah caused Jesus (as) to die the death of sleep and then raised him to the sky, rescuing him from the Jews, who were inflicting suffering upon him at the time." [4]

Imam Muhammad Zahid al-Kawthari, another Islamic scholar who examined the meaning of *tawaffa*, stated that it did not mean death, and drew attention to the use of *mawt* in one verse of the Qur'an:

Had Jesus (as) died [which is not the case], then the word mawt revealed in the verse: **"Allah takes the souls [of people] at death"** *(39:42), would not have been revealed... This is because if, as has been claimed, Allah had referred to normal death [in the biological sense], then this would have been clearly stated. Since Allah refers to the fact that the Jews did not kill Jesus (as), but that he was taken and raised to the sky, then one must think of a meaning beyond that of ordinary death. [5]*

Abu Mansur Muhammad al-Maturidi, regarded as one of the first Qur'anic commentators, also stated that the verse does not refer to Jesus (as) dying in the familiar biological sense:

The thing being referred to in the verse is not passing on in the sense of death, but in the sense of the body being taken from this world. [6]

The famous commentator and scholar, al-Tabari, stated that the verb is used in the sense of "removing from earth" and interpreted the verse in the following terms:

In my opinion, the soundest thing is to take this word in the sense of "to take into one's possession," "draw [away] from earth." In that case, the meaning of the verse is: "I shall take you from earth and into the heavens." The rest of the verse emphasises the [believers'] victory over unbelievers in the End Times, which confirms the above idea." [7]

In his commentary, Hamdi Yazir of Elmali stated that the verse in question means:

In my view, a summary of this interpretation and belief is as follows: The soul of Jesus (as), described as a "word from Allah" and reinforced with the "Purest Spirit", has not yet been taken. His soul has not come to the hour of death. "The Word" has not yet returned to Allah. He still has work to do in this world.[8]

We can conclude from these extensive reference sources that Jesus (as) was placed in a condition similar to sleep and then raised to Allah's presence. Jesus (as) did not die, but was merely removed from this dimension by His will and Allah knows best.

2) *QATALA*: TO KILL

The word generally used for "to kill" when speaking of death in the Qur'an is the Arabic word *qatala*. For example in Surah Ghafir:

Pharaoh said, "Let me kill Musa and let him call upon his Lord! I am afraid that he may change your religion and bring about corruption in the land." (Surah Ghafir: 26)

The expression "let me kill Musa" in the verse appears in the Arabic form *aqtulu Musa*. That word comes from the verb qatala. In another verse, the same word is used in this way:

... (That was because they) killed (yaqtuloona) the Prophets without any right to do so. (Surat al-Baqara: 61)

The words "they killed" in the verse appear as *yaqtuloona* in the original Arabic, which again derives from the verb *qatala*. And as the translation makes quite clear, it means "to kill".

It is clear how the verb *qatala* is used in the following verses that describe the death of prophets. All the words whose meaning appears in brackets derive from the verb *qatala*.

... We will write down what they said and their killing *(wa qatlahum)* of the Prophets without any right to do so... (Surah Al 'Imran: 181)

... Did you grow arrogant, and deny some of them and murder *(taqtuloona)* others? (Surat al-Baqara: 87)

... Say, "Why then, if you are muminun, did you previously kill *(taqtuloona)* the Prophets of Allah?" (Surat al-Baqara: 91)

As for those who reject Allah's Signs, and kill *(yaqtuloona)* the Prophets without any right to do so, and kill *(yaqtuloona)* those who command justice... (Surah Al 'Imran: 21)

... So why did you kill them *(qataltumoohum)* if you are telling the truth? (Surah Al 'Imran: 183)

... The one said, "I shall kill you *(la aqtulannaka)*." ... (Surat al-Ma'ida: 27)

Even if you do raise your hand against me to kill me *(li taqtulanee)*, I am not going to raise my hand against you to kill you *(li aqtulaka)* ... (Surat al-Ma'ida: 28)

"Kill *(uqtuloo)* Yusuf or expel him to some land ..." (Surah Yusuf: 9)

The wife of Pharaoh said, "A source of delight for me and for you; do not kill him *(la taqtuloohu)*..." (Surat al-Qasas: 9)

... "Musa, the Council are conspiring to kill you *(li yaq-tulooka)* ..." (Surat al-Qasas: 20)

The only answer of his (Ibrahim's) people was to say: "Kill *(uqtuloohu)* him or burn him!" (Surat al-'Ankabut: 24)

3) *HALAKA*: TO PERISH

The verb *halaka* is used in the Qur'an meaning "to perish". This verb is used in verses in the sense of "to perish, be destroyed, die". An example of its occurrence can be found in Surah Ghafir:

... when he (Yusuf) died *(halaka)*, you said, "Allah will never send another Messenger after him."... (Surah Ghafir: 34)

In the verse, the expression translated in English as "when he died" is i*dha halaka* in Arabic, used in the sense of "to die".

4) *MAATA*: DEATH

Another word used in the Qur'an in the context of prophets' deaths is *maata*. The word *maata* – he died – and other words from the same root are used in several verses. One of these concerns the death of the Prophet Sulayman (Solomon) (as) in Surah Saba':

Then when We decreed that he should die *(mawt)*, nothing divulged his death *(mawtihi)* to them except the worm which ate his staff ... (Surah Saba': 14)

Another word from the same root is used in reference to the Prophet Yahya (John) (as):

Peace be upon him the day he was born, and the day he
dies *(yamootu)*, and the day he is raised up again alive.
(Surah Maryam: 15)

The word translated here as "when he dies" is the Arabic
word *yamootu*. The same word appears in verses in the context of
the death of the Prophet Ya'qub (Jacob) (as). It appears in Surat
al-Baqara, for instance:

Or were you present when death *(mawt)* came to
Ya'qub? ... (Surat al-Baqara: 133)

The word *mawt* in the verse comes from the same root and
means death. In a verse about the Prophet Muhammad (saas) the
verbs *qutila* and *maata* are used at one and the same time:

Muhammad is only a Messenger and he has been pre-
ceded by other Messengers. If he were to die *(mata)* or
be killed *(qutila)*, would you turn on your heels? ...
(Surah Al 'Imran: 144)

The word *mawt* which comes from the same root as *mata* (to
die) appears in other verses to do with the deaths of prophets:

... She said, "Oh if only I had died *(mittu)* before this
time and was something discarded and forgotten!"
(Surah Maryam: 23)

We did not give any human being before you immortality *(khuld)*. And if you die *(mitta)*, will they then be
immortal? (Surat al-Anbiya': 34)

"He Who will cause my death *(yumeetunee)*, then give
me life." (Surat ash-Shu'ara': 81)

5) *KHALID*: IMMORTAL

Another word that appears in some verses without directly

meaning "to die" or "to kill" but which means "immortality" is *khalid*. The meaning of the word khalid suggests something along the lines of being permanent, for example, in Surat al-Anbiya:

> **We did not give them bodies which did not eat food, nor were they immortal *(khalideena)*. (Surat al-Anbiya': 8)**

6) *SALABA*: TO CRUCIFY

One of the words used in the Qur'an when speaking of the death of prophets and others is the verb *salaba* (to crucify). The verb carries meanings such as "to crucify, hang, and execute". The verb is used in the following verses:

> **... They did not kill him and they did not crucify him *(wa ma salaboohu)*... (Surat an-Nisa': 157)**

> **... (Yusuf said,) One of you will serve his lord with wine, the other of you will be crucified *(yuslabu)*... (Surah Yusuf: 41)**

> **... they should be killed or crucified *(yusallaboo)*... (Surat al-Ma'ida: 33)**

> **(Pharaoh said,) "I will cut off your alternate hands and feet and then I will crucify *(la usallibannakum)* every one of you." (Surat al-A'raf: 124)**

> **... (Pharaoh said,) "I will cut off your hands and feet alternately and have you crucified *(wa la usallibannakum)* ..." (Surah Ta Ha: 71)**

> **... (Pharaoh said,) "I will cut off your alternate hands and feet and I will crucify *(wa la usallibannakum)* every one of you." (Surat ash-Shu'ara': 49)**

As can be seen from these extensive examples, very different words are used in verses dealing with the death of other prophets. Allah has revealed in the Qur'an that Jesus (as) was not killed, that someone who resembled him was shown in his place, and that he was taken back (in other words that his soul was taken). While the word *tawaffa* meaning "to take the soul" is used in the context of Jesus (as), expressions such as, *qataloohu* and *mata*, expressions of normal death, are used to refer to other prophets. These facts demonstrate once again that the situation of Jesus (as) is an extraordinary one.

Allah Raised Jesus (as) to His Presence in Body and Soul

The most undeniable proof that Jesus (as) neither died nor was killed is the fact that Allah has revealed that He raised Jesus (as) to His presence:

"... [I will] raise you up *(rafi'uka)* to Me and purify you of those who are disbelievers. And I will place the people who follow you above those who are disbelievers until the Day of Rising..." (Surah Al 'Imran: 55)

On the contrary *[bal]* Allah raised him up to Himself. Allah is Almighty, All-Wise. (Surat an-Nisa': 158)

Allah protected and rescued Jesus (as) by raising him to His presence. The words *rafiu'ka* and *rafa'ahu* that appear in the verses come from the Arabic root *rafa'a*, which means "to rise".

There is a consensus among Islamic scholars, based on these verses, that Jesus (as) did not die but was raised to Allah's presence, and that this ascension took place in both body and soul.

The Islamic scholar, Abu Musa al-Ash'ari, interpreted Surah

Al 'Imran 55 together with Surat an-Nisa' 158, and wrote that: *"There is a consensus among the community of the faithful [ijma' ummat] that Jesus (as) was raised alive to the heavens."* [9] (*Ijma' ummat* refers to the agreement on this issue of those Islamic scholars who expounded upon Islamic law and lived during the same century).

In his commentary, Hasan Basri Cantay interpreted *rafiu'ka* as meaning "raising and lifting up to Himself," and wrote that *"Allah raised and lifted up Jesus (as) in both body and soul."* [10]

Imam Ibn Taymiyya opined: *The verse "He raised him to His presence" ... explains that Jesus (as) was raised in both body and soul.* [11]

Zahid al-Kawthari stated that the ascension is so clear and certain that there is no room for any objections. Al-Kawthari cited Surah Al 'Imran 55 and Surat an-Nisa' 157-158 as evidence and said that this event is beyond doubt. He uses the word nass, which means certainty or indisputability stemming from a Qur'anic verse or a hadith. He went on to say:

> *That is because the basic meaning of the word (rafa'a in the verses) is transportation from below to above. There is no element here that could be used to interpret the verses metaphorically. Therefore, there is no evidence for seeking to produce a meaning in the sense of ascension in honor and station.* [12]

As clearly seen from the verses and the Islamic scholars' comments, Jesus (as) was raised alive, with his body, to Allah's presence. This is a miracle of Allah, and a wonder that will inspire great enthusiasm and excitement among all believers. Claims that only his soul was raised to His presence, or that his ascension was only spiritual (in station), do not reflect the facts. The invalidity of such claims has been proven by many Islamic scholars as shown above.

Another important proof of this event is the Arabic word *bal*, which appears in Qur'an, 4:158, and has the literal translation of "on the contrary". The features of its meaning and use in Arabic linguistics indicate a very important fact: according to the rules of Arabic linguistics, the sentence that comes after it must have a meaning that is completely opposite to the preceding statement. That being the case, it is likely that the verses referring to Jesus (as) **"... They did not kill him,"** ((Surat an-Nisa': 157) **"on the contrary [*bal*] Allah raised him up to Himself..."** ((Surat an-Nisa': 158) refer to the state of being alive, rather than the state of being dead. Sheikh al-Islam Mustafa Sabri offered the following interpretation:

> *If the term bal, which appears in Surat an-Nisa' 158 and which I have translated as "on the contrary," comes after a sentence expressing a negativity, then, according to the rules of Arabic linguistics, the sentence following it must mean the exact opposite of the one preceding it. The opposite of death is life. This is a requirement of the rules of linguistics. If we say that "the ascension here is a spiritual one" and "Jesus (as) died in the normal sense," then we are violating that rule. In that case, the ascension following the expression "on the contrary" would not represent the opposite to the verbs of "killing" and "crucifying" in the negative sentence preceding it. That is because it may be possible for a person to be killed and for his or her soul to rise to the skies. Otherwise, this term would be meaningless, and there are no meaningless terms in the Qur'an ... According to those who support the thesis that the ascension is only one of the soul, the meaning of the verse is this: "They did not kill him and did not crucify him ... on the contrary, Allah raised his station." There is no particular oratory here, let alone succinctness ... No rational person could take the words "The elevator in my building raises me to the fourth floor*

every day," to mean that I am only raised to the fourth floor in spirit. Therefore, neither was Jesus (as) raised only in spirit. [13]

Said Ramadan al-Buti interpreted the subject in the same way:

The mutual compatibility between the verse's previous and later sections necessarily reveals a fact. For example, if an Arab says: "I am not hungry; on the contrary, I am lying on my side," this is not a correct sentence. In the same way, there is a discrepancy between the components in the sentence: "Khalid did not die; on the contrary, he is a good man." What would be correct is to say: "Khalid did not die; on the contrary, he is alive." To say: "The chairman was not killed; he is a man with a superior station in Allah's presence" also leads to a break in meaning in the sentence, for his having a high station in Allah's sight is no obstacle to his being killed. The term bal expresses a contradiction between the preceding and the following words. In other words, bal cancels out a previous statement. [14]

Clearly, Almighty Allah confounded the unbelievers by raising Jesus (as) alive to His presence. All of this evidence shows that Jesus (as) is still alive and will return to Earth when Allah wills and Allah knows best.

THE RETURN OF JESUS (AS) TO EARTH

The Return of Jesus (as) to Earth in the Qur'an

rom what has been related so far, it is clear that Jesus (as) did not die but was raised to the presence of Allah. However, there is one more point that is underlined by the Qur'an: Jesus (as) will come back to earth.

The Qur'an explicitly declares the return of Jesus (as) to earth and there are several proofs to confirm this:

Proof # 1

Surah Al 'Imran 55 is one of the verses indicating that Jesus (as) will come back:

When Allah said, '"Isa, I will take you back and raise you up to Me and purify you of those who are disbelievers. And I will place the people who follow you above those who are disbelievers until the Day of Rising. Then you will all return to Me, and I will judge between you regarding the things about which you differed. (Surah Al 'Imran: 55)

The statement in the verse, "**And I will place the people** who follow you above those who are disbelievers until the Day of Rising" is important. Here, there is reference to a group strictly adhering to Jesus (as) and who will be kept above the disbelievers until the Day of Judgement. Who are these adherents, then? Are they the disciples who lived in the time of Jesus or are they the Christians of today?

Before he was raised up to Allah, the followers of Jesus (as) were few. After his ascension, the essence of the true religion degenerated rapidly. Furthermore, the disciples faced serious pressure throughout their lives. During the succeeding two centuries, having no political power, those Christians having faith in Jesus (as) were also oppressed. In this case, it is not possible to say that early Christians or their successors during these periods were physically superior to the disbelievers in the world. We might logically think that this verse does not refer to them.

When we look at the Christians of today, on the other hand, we notice that the essence of Christianity has changed significantly and it is markedly different from what Jesus (as) originally brought to mankind. Christians embraced the perverted belief that suggests that Jesus (as) is the son of God and similarly held the doctrine of the Trinity (the Father, Son and the Holy Spirit). (Surely Allah is beyond that.) In this case, it is flawed to accept the Christians of today as the adherents of the true religion revealed to Jesus (as). In many verses of the Qur'an Allah states that the belief of the Trinity is a perverted one:

Those who say that the Messiah, son of Maryam, is the third of three are disbelievers. There is no god but One God. (Surat al-Ma'ida: 73)

In this case, the commentary of the statement, "And I will place the people who follow you above those who are disbelievers until the Day of Rising" is as follows: first, it is said that these people are the Muslims who are the only true followers of the authentic teachings of Jesus (as); second, it is said that these people are the Christians, whether or not they hold idolatrous beliefs, and that could be seen to be confirmed by the dominant position that nominal Christians hold on the earth today. However, both positions will be unified by the arrival of Jesus (as), since he will abolish the jizyah (the defence tax payable by non-Muslims living under Muslim rule), meaning that he will not accept that Christians and Jews live with any other religion than Islam, and so will unite all the believers as Muslims.

The Prophet and last Messenger of Allah (saas), has also given the glad tidings of the return of Jesus (as). The scholars of hadith say that the hadiths on this subject, in which Allah's Messenger (saas) said that the Prophet Jesus (as) will descend amongst people as a leader before the Day of Judgement have reached the status of *mutawattir*. That means that they have been narrated by so many people from each generation from such a large group of the Companions that there can be no possible doubt of their authenticity. For example:

> *Abu Hurairah narrated that Allah's Messenger (saas) said, "By the One in Whose hand is my self, definitely the son of Maryam will soon descend among you as a just judge, and he will break the cross, kill the pig and abolish the jizyah, and wealth will be so abundant that no one will accept it, until a single prostration will be better than the world and everything in it. (Sahih Bukhari)*

> *Jabir ibn 'Abdullah said, "I heard the Prophet (saas) saying, 'A party of my ummah will never stop fighting for the truth victoriously until the Day of Rising.' He said, 'Then 'Isa ibn Maryam, peace be upon him, will descend and their amir will say, "Come and lead us in*

prayer," but he will say, "No! some of you are amirs over others," as Allah's showing honour to this ummah.'" (Sahih Muslim)

Abu Hurairah narrated, "The Prophet (saas) said: 'There is no prophet between me and him, that is, 'Isa, peace be upon him. He will descend (to the earth). When you see him, recognise him: a man of medium height, reddish fair, wearing two light yellow garments, looking as if drops were falling down from his head though it will not be wet. He will fight the people for the cause of Islam. He will break the cross, kill the pig, and abolish the jizyah. Allah will cause to perish all religions except Islam. He will destroy the Dajjal and will live on the earth for forty years and then he will die. The Muslims will pray over him.'" (Abu Dawud)

Proof # 2

Earlier in this section, we analysed verses 157-158 of Surat an-Nisa'. Just after these verses Allah states the following in Surat an-Nisa 159:

There is not one of the People of the Book who will not believe in him before he dies; and on the Day of Rising he will be a witness against them. (Surat an-Nisa': 159)

The statement above **"who will not believe in him before he dies"** is important. The Arabic text of this sentence reads: Wa-in min ahli'l-kitabi illa la yuminanna bihi qabla mawtihi.

Some scholars stated that the "him/it" in this verse is used for the Qur'an and thus made the following interpretation: There will be no one from the People of the Book who will not have faith in the Qur'an before he (a person from the People of the Book) dies.

Nevertheless, in verses 157 and 158, which are the two verses preceding this verse, the same "him" is undoubtedly used for Jesus (as).

The verses state:

And (on account of) their saying, "We killed the Messiah, 'Isa son of Maryam, Messenger of Allah." They did not kill him and they did not crucify him but it was made to seem so to them. Those who argue about him are in doubt about it. They have no real knowledge of it, just conjecture. But they certainly did not kill him. (Surat an-Nisa': 157)

Allah raised him up to Himself. Allah is Almighty, All-Wise. (Surat an-Nisa': 158)

Just after these verses in Surat an-Nisa 159, there is no evidence indicating that "him" is used to imply someone or something other than Jesus (as).

There is not one of the People of the Book who will not believe in him before he dies; and on the Day of Rising he will be a witness against them. (Surat an-Nisa': 159)

In the Qur'an, Allah informs us that on the Day of Judgement, the **"tongues and hands and feet will testify against them about what they were doing"** (Surat an-Nur: 24 and Surah Yasin: 65). From Surah Fussilat 20-23, we learn that **"hearing, sight and skin will testify against us."** In none of the verses however, is there reference to the Qur'an as a witness. If we accept that the "him" or "it" in the first sentence refers to the Qur'an – though grammatically or logically we have no evidence whatsoever – then we should also accept that the "he" in the second statement also refers to the Qur'an. To accept this however, there should be an explicit verse confirming this view.

In addition, the words **"... Allah raised him up to Himself"** in the preceding verse once again shows that it is not the Qur'an that is being indicated in this verse. The Qur'an has been a guidance for the faithful for the last 1400 years, and has not been raised up to Allah. It is Jesus (as) who has been raised up to Him. This is yet another proof that the witnessing referred to in the verse is that of Jesus (as) for the People of the Book, and that the pronoun "he" in the verse does not refer to the Qur'an.

In other verses, we see that when the same personal pronoun is used for the Qur'an, there is generally mention of the Qur'an before or after that specific verse as in the cases of Surat an-Naml: 77 and Surat ash-Shu'ara: 192-196. The verse straightforwardly defines that People of the Book will have faith in Jesus (as) and that he (Jesus (as)) will be a witness against them.

The second point is about the interpretation of the expression "before he dies". Some think this is having faith in Jesus (as) before their own death. According to this interpretation everyone from the People of the Book will definitely believe in Jesus (as) before they face their own death. Arabic linguistics, however, shows that this claim is not correct. The plural suffix *hum* is used in all those verses of the Qur'an that refer to the People of the Book (as in Surat al-Bayyina 1 and 6, Surat al-Hadid 29, and Surat al-Hashr 2). Yet the singular suffix *hu* is employed in this verse. This means that the verse reports that the People of the Book will believe in Jesus (as) before his death – in other words, before his biological death at his second coming. Besides, in Jesus' (as) time Jews who are defined as the People of the Book not only did not have faith in Jesus (as) but also attempted to kill him. On the other hand, it is not possible to say that Jews and Christians who lived and died after the time of Jesus had faith – the type of faith described in the Qur'an – in him.

To conclude, when we make a careful evaluation of the verse, we arrive at the following conclusion: Before Jesus' (as) death, all the People of the Book will have faith in him. [15]

Therefore, it is evident that firstly, the verse refers to the future because there is mention of the death of Jesus (as). Yet, Jesus (as) did not die but was raised up to the presence of Allah. Jesus (as) will come to earth again, he will live for a specified time and then die. Secondly, all the People of the Book will have faith in him. This is an event which has yet not occurred, but which will happen in the future.

Consequently, by the expression "before he dies", there is a reference to Jesus (as). The People of the Book will see him, know him and obey him while he is alive. Meanwhile, Jesus (as) will bear witness against them on the Last Day and Allah knows best.

Proof # 3

That Jesus (as) will come back to earth towards the end of time is related in another verse of the Qur'an.

When an example is made of <u>the son of Maryam ('Isa)</u> your people laugh uproariously. They retort, "Who is better then, our gods or him?" They only say this to you for argument's sake. They are indeed a disputatious people.

<u>He is only a slave</u> on whom We bestowed Our blessing and whom We made an example for the tribe of Israel.

If We wished, We could appoint angels in exchange for you to succeed you on the earth. (Surat az-Zukhruf: 57-60)

Just after these verses, Allah declares that Jesus (as) is a sign of the Day of Judgement.

He is a Sign of the Hour. Have no doubt about it. But follow me. This is a straight path. (Surat az-Zukhruf: 61)

Ibn Juzayy says that the first meaning of this verse is that Jesus (as) is a sign or a precondition of the Last Hour. We can say that this verse informs us that Jesus (as) will come back to earth at the end times. That is because Jesus (as) lived approximately six centuries before the revelation of the Qur'an. Consequently, we cannot interpret his first coming as a sign of the Day of Judgement. What this verse actually indicates is that Jesus (as) will come back to earth towards the end of time and this will be a sign for the Day of Judgement.

The Arabic of the verse "He is a Sign of the Hour" is *Innahu la 'ilmun li's-sa'ati...* Some people interpret the pronoun hu in this verse as the Qur'an. However, the preceding verses explicitly indicate that Jesus (as) is mentioned in the verse: "He is only a slave on whom We bestowed Our blessing and whom We made an example for the tribe of Israel." [16]

Those who cite this pronoun as referring to the Qur'an go on to quote the next part of the verse "Have no doubt about it. But follow me" as so-called evidence. However, the verses preceding this one refer completely to Jesus (as). For this reason, it appears that the pronoun hu is linked to those preceding verses and also refers to Jesus (as). In fact, great Islamic scholars declare that to be the case, based on the use of the pronoun both in the Qur'an and in the hadith.

Among contemporary Islamic scholars, Sayyid Qutb drew attention to the important evidence concerning Jesus' (as) second coming, in his commentary:

Many hadith regard Jesus' (as) descent to earth prior to the Day of

Judgment. Indeed, the verse, "He is a Sign of the Hour" also indicates this. In other words, Jesus (as) will descend to earth at a time close to the Day of Judgment. In a second style of reading, the verse reads "wa innahu la 'ilmun li al-saa'ati." In other words, his descent is a sign, a sign of the Day of Judgment. Both styles of reading express the same meaning. His descent from the skies is a news of the Unseen World, spoken of by the right-speaking and trustworthy Prophet (saas) and indicated in the glorious Qur'an. Apart from the information from these two sources, which will remain unchanged until the Day of Judgment, nobody can say anything else about the subject. [17]

Al-Kawthari stated that even in the oldest doctrinal texts, this verse was used as evidence of Jesus' (as) return. [18] Omer Nasuhi Bilmen explained the verse in these terms:

It gives news, in an indubitable manner, that Jesus (as) is a sign of the approach of the Day of Judgment and that the Day of Judgment will certainly come ... His appearance on earth is regarded as a law of the Last Day... [19]

In fact, this title is unique to Jesus (as), for although the Qur'an describes the lives of Prophet Muhammad (saas), Ibrahim (Abraham) (as), Nuh (Noah) (as), Musa (Moses) (as), Sulayman (Solomon) (as), Yusuf (Joseph) (as), Dawud (David) (as), Yaqub (Jacob) (as), and a great many other prophets, this title is applied to none of them. This fact is yet another indication that Jesus (as) possesses a special feature that the other prophets do not: He will return to Earth after having been raised to Allah's presence and Allah knows best.

Proof # 4

Other verses indicating the second coming of the Jesus (as)

are as follows:

> When the angels said, "Maryam, your Lord gives you good news of a Word from Him. His name is the Messiah, 'Isa, son of Maryam of high esteem in this world and the hereafter, and one of those brought near. He will speak to people in the cradle, and also when fully grown, and will be one of the righteous," she said, "My Lord! How can I have a son when no man has ever touched me?"

> He said, "It will be so. Allah creates whatever He wills. When He decides on something He just says to it, 'Be!' and it is. He will <u>teach him the Book</u> and Wisdom, and the Tawrah and the Injil..." (Surah Al 'Imran: 45-48)

In this verse, it is heralded that Allah will instruct Jesus (as) about the *Injil*, the Tawrah and the "Book." We come across the same expression in the Surat al-Ma'ida:

> Remember when Allah said: "'Isa, son of Maryam, remember My blessing to you and to your mother when I reinforced you with the Purest Spirit so that you could speak to people in the cradle and when you were fully grown; and when I taught you the Book and Wisdom, and the Tawrah and the Injil; and when you created a bird-shape out of clay by My permission..." (Surat al-Ma'idah: 110)

When we analyse the "Book" in both of the verses, we see that it may indicate the Qur'an. In the verses, it is stated that the Qur'an is the last divine book sent apart from the *Tawrah*, the *Zabur* and the *Injil*. Besides, in another verse in the Qur'an, next to the Tawrah and the Injil, the word "Book" is used to indicate the Qur'an.

Allah, there is no god but Him, the Living, the Self-Sustaining. He has sent down the Book to you with truth, confirming what has there before it. And He sent down the Tawrah and the Injil, previously... (Surah Al 'Imran: 2-3)

Some other verses in which "Book" refers to the Qur'an state:

When a Book does come to them from Allah, confirming what is with them – even though before that they were praying for victory over the unbelievers – yet when what they recognise does come to them, they reject it. Allah's curse is on the unbelievers. (Surat al-Baqara: 89)

For this We sent a Messenger to you from among you to recite Our Signs to you and purify you and teach you the Book and Wisdom and teach you things you did not know before. (Surat al-Baqara: 151)

In this case, it is clear that the third book that will be taught to Jesus (as) will be the Qur'an and that this will be possible only if he comes to earth at the end of time. Jesus (as) lived approximately six hundred years before the revelation of the Qur'an. Besides, it is another piece of evidence that the hadiths of the Prophet Muhammad (saas) inform that when the Prophet Jesus (as) comes for the second time, he will command with the Qur'an, not the *Injil*:

He will lead you according to the Book of your Lord and the Sunnah of your Apostle. (Sahih Muslim)

As this expression clearly shows, when Jesus (as) returns to earth, he will rule with the commandments of the Qur'an and will maintain the Sunnah of the Prophet Muhammed (saas), a hadith which is in agreement with the Qur'anic verses.

Another important piece of information is that the term revealed for Jesus (as) was not revealed for any other prophet. For example, the Qur'an reveals that the *Tawrah* was given to Musa (Moses) (as), that *Suhuf* (Pages) were given to Ibrahim (Abraham) (as), and that the Book of Psalms was given to Dawud (David) (as). If there were books revealed before the prophets' own time, the Qur'an states that they knew them. However, only in the case of Jesus does the Qur'an state that a prophet will be taught a book that was revealed after his own time. This is one of the indications that he will return to earth and that when he does so, he will rule with the book revealed after his lifetime: the Qur'an.

Proof # 5

Allah tells about the ascension of Jesus (as) in Surah Maryam as follows:

('Isa said,) Peace be upon me the day I was born, and the day I die and the day I am raised up again alive. (Surah Maryam: 33)

When we consider this verse together with Surah Al 'Imran 55, it indicates a very important truth. In the verse in Surah Al 'Imran it is stated that Jesus (as) was raised up to the presence of Allah. No information is given in this verse about death or killing. Yet in Surah Maryam: 33 information is given about the day when Jesus (as) will die. That second death can only be possible if Jesus (as) dies after returning to and living on earth and only Allah knows for certain.

Proof # 6

Another piece of evidence about Jesus (as) returning to earth appears in Surat al-Ma'ida and in Surah Al 'Imran in the form of the word *kahlan*. The verses say:

> **Remember when Allah said, "'Isa, son of Maryam, remember My blessing to you and to your mother when I reinforced you with the Purest Ruh (Spirit) so that you could speak to people in the cradle and when you were fully grown *(kahlan)*... (Surat al-Ma'ida: 110)**

> **He will speak to people in the cradle, and also when fully grown *(kahlan)*, and will be one of the righteous. (Surah Al 'Imran: 46)**

This word appears only in the above two verses in the Qur'an, and only in reference to Jesus (as). The meaning of the word *kahlan*, used to refer to Jesus' (as) adult state, is along the lines of between thirty and fifty years old, someone who is no longer young, someone who has reached the perfect age. Islamic scholars agree on translating this word as indicating the period after thirty-five years of age.

Based on a hadith reported by Ibn 'Abbas to the effect that Jesus (as) ascended to heaven in his early thirties, at a young age, and will stay another forty years when he returns, Islamic scholars say that Jesus' old age will be after he returns to earth. [20]

In looking at the verses of the Qur'an, we see that this statement is only used for Jesus (as). All the prophets spoke to people and called them to the true path. They all communicated their message in maturity. Yet there is no such statement in the Qur'an about any other prophet. The statement is only used to refer to Jesus (as) and indicates his miraculous situation. That is because the words "in the cradle" and "when fully grown" that follow each other in the verses are stressing two miraculous periods.

In fact, in his work *The Commentary of at-Tabari*, Imam at-Tabari gives the following explanation of these verses:

> *These statements (Surat al-Ma'ida, 110) indicate that in order to complete his lifespan and speak to people when fully grown Jesus (as) will come down from heaven. That is because he was raised to heaven when still young. In this verse (Surah Al 'Imran, 46) there is evidence that Jesus is living, and Ahl al-Sunnah share that view. That is because in this verse it is stated that he will speak to people when fully grown. He will only be able to grow fully when he returns to earth from heaven.* [21]

Some people however, interpret the word "when fully grown" in a manner far removed from its true meaning and do not analyse it in the context of the general logic of the Qur'an. These people maintain that prophets have always been mature adults, for which reason the expression refers to all the lives of the prophets. Of course the prophets were mature adults whom Allah raised. Yet in Surat al-Ahqaf Allah reveals that the age of full maturity is forty. It is revealed in this verse that:

We have instructed man to be good to his parents. His mother bore him with difficulty and with difficulty gave birth to him; and his bearing and weaning take thirty months. Then when he achieves his full strength and reaches forty, he says, "My Lord, keep me thankful for the blessing You bestowed on me and on my parents, and keep me acting rightly, pleasing You. And make my descendants righteous. I have repented to You and I am truly one of the Muslims." (Surat al-Ahqaf: 15)

The word *kahlan*, therefore, also points to Jesus' (as) return to earth just like all the other information given in the Qur'an and only Allah knows for certain.

As seen, verses on Jesus' (as) return to the earth are very explicit. Similar expressions to these are not used in the Qur'an regarding other prophets. All these expressions, however, are used about the Prophet Jesus (as), which suggests that his situation is unique and miraculous.

There Are Other Examples of People in the Qur'an Who Left the World and Then Returned After Hundreds of Years

A man who was resurrected after a century

The Qur'an gives the example of a man who remained dead for a century. This is related in Surat al-Baqara:

> Or the one who passed by a town which had fallen into ruin? He asked, "How can Allah restore this to life when it has died?" Allah caused him to die a hundred years then brought him back to life. Then He asked, "How long have you been here?" He replied, "I have been here a day or part of a day." He said, "Not so! You have been here a hundred years. Look at your food and drink – it has not gone bad – and look at your donkey so We can make you a Sign for all mankind. Look at the bones – how We raise them up and clothe them in flesh." When it had become clear to him, he said, "Now I know that Allah has power over all things." (Surat al-Baqara: 259)

In the verses given in the previous pages, there is mention of the fact that Jesus (as) did not die but was "taken back." In the verse above, the man, however, definitely died. Consequently, even a dead person can rise again by the will of Allah and the above verse states this explicitly.

The Companions of the Cave awoke after years

The story of the "Companions of the Cave" is related in Surat al-Kahf. These were young men who were compelled to take refuge from the cruel tyranny of the ruler of the time in a cave. It is related that they fell asleep and were woken up after years of sleep:

> When the young men took refuge in the cave and said, "Our Lord, give us mercy directly from You and open the way for us to right guidance in our situation." So We sealed their ears with sleep in the cave for a number of years. (Surat al-Kahf: 10-11)

> You would have supposed them to be awake whereas in fact they were asleep. We moved them to the right and to the left, and at the entrance, their dog stretched out its paws. If you had looked down and seen them, you would have turned from them and run and have been filled with terror at the sight of them.

> That was the situation when we woke them up so they could question one another. One of them asked, "How long have you been here?" They replied "We have been here for a day or part of a day." They said, "Your Lord knows best how long have you been here. Send one of your number into the city with this silver you have, so he can see which food is purest and bring you some of it to eat. But he should go about with caution so that no

one is aware of you." (Surat al-Kahf: 18-19)

The Qur'an does not explain exactly how much time the young men spent in the cave. Instead, the duration of this period is implied by the words "for a number of years". People's guess at this period however was rather high: three hundred and nine years. Allah says:

They stayed in their Cave for three hundred years and added nine. Say: "Allah knows best how long they stayed. The Unseen of the heavens and the earth belongs to Him. How perfectly He sees, how well He hears! They have no protector apart from Him. Nor does He share His rule with anyone." (Surat al-Kahf: 25-26)

Under normal conditions, people obviously cannot sleep for such a long period. This sleep, therefore, may not be the type of sleep with which we are familiar. Perhaps they were taken into another dimension, one in which time and space do not apply, and were later sent back to earth.

Just like people waking up from sleep, these people also returned to life. In a similar way, Jesus (as) will return to life when he comes back to earth and, after fulfilling the honorable responsibility imposed on him by Allah, and, as a requirement of the verse; **He said: "On it [earth] you will live and on it die, and from it you will be brought forth,"** (Surat al-A'raf: 25) he will die on earth, like every other human being and Allah knows best.

The Return of Jesus (as) to Earth in the Hadith

The fact that Jesus (as) is alive in Allah's presence and that he will return to earth in the end times appears in some detail in the hadith collections, among them al-Shaybani's *Taysir al-Usul ila Jami' al-Usul;* Imam Maliki's *Al-Muwatta';* the Sahihs of Ibn Khuzayma and Ibn Hibban; and the Musnads of Ibn Hanbal and al-Tayalisi, regarded as the greatest sources of the most reliable hadith. We present a selection of these hadiths:

> *Jesus (as), son of Mary, will definitely descend as a just judge and a just ruler. (Imam Nawawi, Commentary on Sahih Muslim)*

> *Doomsday will not take place until Jesus, son of Maryam, (as) comes as a fair ruler and a just imam. (Sunan Ibn Majah)*

> *By Him in Whose Hands my soul is, the son of Maryam (Jesus [as]) will shortly descend among you people as a just ruler. (Sahih Bukhari)*

> *There is no prophet between him (Jesus [as]) and me. He will certainly descend. Recognise him when you see him. He is of medium height, of a reddish white color. He will wear two sets of yellow dyed clothing. Water will fall from his hair even if it does not rain. He will fight with people for Islam. He will slay the Antichrist and then remain for exactly forty years on Earth. Then he will die, and Muslims will perform the prayers for him. (Sahih Bukhari and Sahih Muslim)*

> *What will you do when the son of Maryam (as) descends among you and leads as one amongst you? (Sahih Muslim)*

> *Jesus, son of Maryam, (as) will then descend and their [the Muslims'] commander will invite him to come and lead them in prayer. But he will say: "No, some among you are commanders over some [among you.]" (Sahih Muslim)*

Furthermore, many Islamic scholars have carried out research and studies on these facts and have written books and treatises on them. These are also invaluable sources. Heading the list of these great Islamic scholars is Abu Hanifa, the founder of the Hanafi legal school. In the final chapter of his book *Al-Fiqh al-Akbar*, Abu Hanifa states:

> *The emergence of the Antichrist and of Gog and Magog is a reality; the rising of the Sun in the west is a reality; the descent of Jesus, upon whom be peace, from the heavens is a reality; and all of the other signs of the Day of Resurrection, as contained in the authentic traditions, are established realities.* [22]

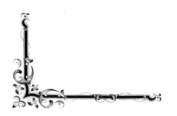

HOW CAN WE RECOGNISE JESUS (AS)?

Who Will Be Able to Recognise Jesus (as)?

*J*t has been established in the light of the Qur'an, hadith and the interpretations of Islamic scholars that Jesus (as) did not die and was raised up to the presence of Allah and that he will indeed come back to earth. However, one question remains: How will we recognise Jesus (as) when he comes back to the world and which of his attributes will make him recognisable?

The Qur'an, either in the verses or in particular stories, provides us detailed information regarding the prophets' lives and superior morality. Many common attributes of the prophets and of the true believers are mentioned in the Qur'an. Accordingly, referring to the Qur'an and the Sunnah, sincere believers can identify these superior attributes and accordingly recognise Jesus (as).

However, very few people will recognise Jesus (as) when he returns, as stated by Bediuzzaman Said Nursi:

When Jesus (as) comes, it is not necessary that everyone should know him to be the true Jesus. His elect and those close to him will recognise him through the light of belief. It will not be self-evident so that everyone will recognise him. [23]

As Said Nursi says, during the early years of his second coming, the people that know of Jesus (as) will be limited to a small group of people who are close to him. Furthermore, this will only be possible by the 'light of belief'. 'The light of belief' is the comprehension granted by Allah to those who believe in the existence and unity of Allah, observe the commands of the Qur'an and live by the Sunnah of the Messenger of Allah, Muhammad (saas). With such comprehension, believers can evaluate situations precisely and grasp the details of events with no difficulty. As the Qur'an informs us, believers are those people who ponder upon everything surrounding them and thus never miss the details or subtle aspects of things. Indeed, Allah informs man that He will grant discrimination to judge between right and wrong *(Al-Furqan)* to those who reflect upon matters in the hope of comprehending the greatness and might of Allah and to those who have fear *(taqwa)* of Him:

You who believe! If you have taqwa of Allah, He will give you discrimination and erase your bad actions from you and forgive you. Allah's favour is indeed immense. (Surat al-Anfal: 29)

Thus, those who will recognise Jesus (as) during his second coming and adhere to his message will actually be the righteous believers who believe in Allah and the Qur'an and in the Messenger of Allah (saas) and think deeply over things. Bediuzzaman Said Nursi, too, draws attention to this issue as follows:

In fact, although when Jesus (as) comes he himself will know he is Jesus, not everyone will know. [24]

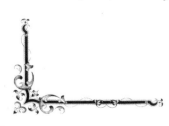

Which Attributes of Jesus (as) Make Him Recognisable?

In answering this question, we first refer to the Qur'an in search of those attributes that are common to all the prophets related in the Qur'an and this would be equally applicable to Jesus (as). In fact, there are numerous attributes of prophets but in this section we will emphasise the most apparent ones that are immediately evident.

1. He is different from other people because of his exceptional moral values

Like all other prophets Allah has chosen to proclaim His message to mankind, Jesus (as) is known for his excellent moral values. The most distinctive attribute of Jesus (as) is his exemplary person, immediately discernible in the society he lives in. He, indeed, has an exemplary character, unprecedented in nature and striking to anyone at first sight. He is an extremely committed, courageous and strong person; a manifestation of the trust he puts in Allah and his pure faith in Him. With such traits, he has a profound influence on everyone. This superiority, a shared attribute of all prophets, is related in the verse:

> This is the argument We gave to Ibrahim (Abraham) against his people. We raise in rank anyone We will. Your Lord is All-Wise, All-Knowing. We gave him Ishaq (Isaac) and Ya'qub (Jacob), each of whom We guided. And before him We had guided Nuh (Noah). And among his descendants were Dawud (David) and Sulayman (Solomon), and Ayyub (Job), Yusuf (Joseph), Musa (Moses) and Harun (Aaron). That is how We rec-

ompense the good-doers. And Zakarriyya (Zachariah), Yahya (John), 'Isa (Jesus) and Ilyas (Elijah). All of them were among the right-acting. And Isma'il (Ishmael), al-Yasa' (Elisha), Yunus (Jonah) and Lut (Lot). All of them We favoured over all beings. And some of their fore-bears, descendants and brothers; We chose them and guided them to a straight path. (Surat al-An'am: 83-87)

That Allah granted superior attributes to the prophets is expressed precisely in the verse above. There are many other examples narrated in the Qur'an and the verses below inform us of the superior traits granted to the various prophets:

Ibrahim was a community in himself. (Surat an-Nahl: 120)

And remember Our slaves Ibrahim (Abraham), Ishaq (Isaac) and Ya'qub (Jacob), men of true strength and inner sight. (Surah Sad: 45)

In Our eyes they are among the best of chosen men. (Surah Sad: 47)

We gave knowledge to Dawud (David) and Sulayman (Solomon) who said, 'Praise be to Allah who has favoured us over many of His slaves who are believers...' (Surat an-Naml: 15)

Jesus (as) is also one of the chosen prophets of Allah. Allah states the following about him:

These Messengers: We favoured some of them over others. Allah spoke directly to some of them and raised up some of them in rank. We gave clear Signs to 'Isa, son of Maryam, and reinforced him with the Purest Spirit. (Surat al-Baqara: 253)

2. He will be recognised by the expression on his face which is only seen in Prophets

Allah informs us in the Qur'an that the superiority of those whom He has chosen can be in terms of their knowledge and as well as in terms of physical strength:

... He said, "Allah has chosen him over you and favoured him greatly in knowledge and physical strength. Allah gives kingship to anyone He wills. Allah is All Encompassing, All-Knowing. (Surat al-Baqara: 247)

Granted with wisdom, physical strength, knowledge and perfection of character, Jesus (as) will have a unique appearance that is only seen in prophets. His strong fear of Allah and the light of his steadfast faith will all be apparent in his face. This expression on his face will at once distinguish him from others and people who see him will immediately notice that they are meeting someone quite superior. However, not everyone will be able to see this evident truth. Out of anger and pride, it is likely that some people will disregard this superiority and despite feeling it deep inside, they may feign ignorance. Only those having sincere faith will comprehend this superiority and have an appreciation of it.

Allah informs us that Jesus (as) is **"of high esteem in the world and the Hereafter, and one of those brought near..."** (Surah Al 'Imran: 45). Thus, Jesus (as) will be known to those people surrounding him for the honour and excellence only seen in those chosen by Allah.

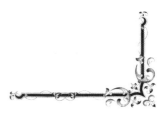

3. He has outstanding wisdom and decisive speech

They are the ones to whom we gave the Book, Judgement, and Prophethood... (Surat al-An'am: 89)

Throughout history, Allah communicated His messages and revelations through His messengers. He also granted wisdom to these messengers: a decisive and highly pertinent style of speaking, exemplary manners in enjoining right actions and in forbidding evil, are all attributes common to the prophets. In the Qur'an, Allah also draws attention to the wisdom granted to each prophet. For instance, for the Prophet Dawud (David) (as), Allah states: **"... We gave him wisdom and decisive speech."** (Surah Sad: 20). Similarly, for the Prophet Yahya (John) (as): **"Yahya, ... We gave him judgement while still a child."** (Surah Maryam: 12) About Musa (Moses) (as), Allah informs us: **"And when he reached his full strength and maturity, We gave him judgement and knowledge."** (Surat al-Qasas: 14). About Luqman: **"We gave Luqman wisdom: 'Give thanks to Allah.'** (Surah Luqman: 12). Similarly, Allah relates: **"We gave the family of Ibrahim the Book and Wisdom..."** (Surat an-Nisa: 54)

Thus another attribute of the prophets is that they have been granted an outstanding wisdom and this would also hold true for Jesus (as) as we learn from the Qur'an:

Remember when Allah said, "'Isa, son of Maryam, remember My blessing to you and to your mother when I reinforced you with the Purest Spirit so that you could speak to people in the cradle and when you were fully grown; and when I taught you the Book and Wisdom, and the Torah and the Injil. (Surat al-Ma'ida: 110)

And when 'Isa came with the Clear Signs, he said, "I have come to you with Wisdom and to clarify for you some of the things about which you have differed. Therefore have taqwa of Allah and obey me." (Surat az-Zukhruf: 63)

These verses show that Jesus (as) will be recognisable by his decisive, highly pertinent and striking speech. As in all other issues, a decisive manner of speaking is an attribute common to the prophets. Believers who adhere to the Qur'an as a guide to the truth grasp that the speech of Jesus (as) has wisdom exclusive to messengers chosen by Allah. The wisdom he displays, the flawless diagnoses he makes, the intelligent solutions he brings will be the clear signs of a special gift that Allah granted to him. Thus, his superiority will be even more evident.

4. He will be very faithful

Each messenger introduced himself to the community to whom they were sent by saying: **"I am a faithful Messenger to you."** (Surat ash-Shua'ra: 107). This faithfullness of the messengers is an outcome of their strict adherence to the Book and religion of Allah and to the obligations set by Him. They meticulously observe the boundaries of Allah and never deviate from His righteous path. Only intending to attain the good pleasure of Allah, they never submit to anyone's desires. The Qur'an informs us that just about all the prophets identified themselves to their peoples by way of this characteristic of theirs. For instance, in the Qur'an, Musa (Moses) (as) introduced himself to the community among whom he lived, as follows:

Before them We put Pharaoh's people to the test when a noble Messenger came to them, saying, "Hand over to

me the slaves of Allah. I am a trustworthy Messenger to you." (Surat ad-Dukhan: 17-18)

No doubt, the communities generally failed to appreciate this important attribute of the messengers. Furthermore, declining to abandon the ignorant way of living in which they indulged and refusing to live by the true religion to which the messengers summoned them, they usually showed intolerance towards them. Only after some time did they perceive the messengers to be trustworthy. Prophet Yusuf (Joseph) (as) is a good example. He was tested with difficulties for an extended period; first he was sold as a slave and then imprisoned for a number of years. By the will of Allah, when the due time arrived, however, he was recognised as a trustworthy person by people, and the king put him in charge of the state treasury:

The King said, "Bring him to me straight away! So I may draw him very close to me." When he had spoken with him, he declared, "Today you are trusted, established in our sight!" (Surah Yusuf: 54)

These attributes of the prophets mentioned in the Qur'an will also be observable in Jesus (as). On his second coming to the earth, as a never-changing law of Allah, he will be known for his trustworthiness. Allah will provide His help to him, as He did to all the other prophets and his trustworthiness will be made manifest in due course.

5. He will be under the protection of Allah

Our Word was given before to Our slaves, the Messengers, that they would certainly be helped. It is Our army which will be victorious. (Surat as-Saffat: 171-173)

Allah granted protection to His messengers over other people. He gave them the might to defeat their enemies and protected them against all their plots. Be it at the stage of taking a decision or putting a plan into practice, Allah always supported them.

Another sign for believers who are waiting for Jesus (as), the Messenger of Allah, is his gift of making everything he does a success. His judgements, for instance, or the methods he employs, all bring remarkable results for himself as well as to the people around him. Truly, some events appearing to be against the good of the public will soon prove to be just the contrary. Such occurrences will indicate the pertinence of his judgements. That is because Allah assures his Messengers that, under all circumstances, they will prevail. So this second coming of Jesus (as) will be very different from the first, since the second will be under the victorious banner of Islam. This promise ensures the overall success Jesus (as) will attain in his mission.

Indeed, this will be so clear that it will inevitably attract the attention of the believers following him. Meanwhile, his enemies will notice the extraordinary nature of this situation as well. However, they will fail to recognise that this is the clear guidance of Allah. That is simply because their main objective in life is to overcome this distinguished person whom they see as an ordinary human being like themselves. However, as stated in the verse, **"Then We will rescue Our Messengers and those who have faith as well. It is incumbent upon Us to rescue the believers."** (Surah Yunus: 103) Allah will render all their efforts useless and help His messenger. The plots made or the struggles waged against him will never succeed.

6. He will not ask for any reward in return for his services

All the prophets referred to in the Qur'an rendered their services in the way of Allah without asking for any reward in return. The only gain they asked was the good pleasure of Allah. No worldly gain, no benefit did they request from anyone. One of the verses extolling this virtue of the Messengers is as follows:

My people! I do not ask for a wage for it. My wage is the responsibility of Him who brought me into being. So will you not use your intellect? (Surah Hud: 51)

This virtue common to all the messengers will also be apparent in Jesus (as). In his second coming, he will call people all over the world to the true religion of Allah. Yet, he will desire no worldly gain in return. Like all other messengers referred in the Qur'an, he will pursue Allah's good pleasure desiring to be rewarded by Him. This trait of his will earn him a reputation in society. Yet, one should also keep in mind that, as in all other aspects, only the believers will recognise and treasure this trait of his. Furthermore, although his enemies recognise him, it is completely possible that they may spread slanders about him, just like those experienced by other prophets in the past. Still, Allah will prove the groundless nature of these slanders and help him, just as He guides him in all his deeds.

7. He will be compassionate and full of mercy towards the believers

Another attribute peculiar to the messengers is their "compassionate and merciful" nature towards the believers. Being gentle and merciful to the believers following them, all the messengers strove to improve the characters of the believers for their well-being both in this world and the next. The most distinctive attribute of Jesus (as) will be his mercy towards the believers. Allah relates this virtue as exemplified in the Last of the Messengers Muhammad (saas), but which is common to all messengers, as follows:

A Messenger has come to you from among yourselves. Your suffering is distressing to him; he is deeply concerned for you; he is gentle and merciful to the believers. (Surat at-Tawbah: 128)

Jesus (as) will also have "deep concern" for the believers surrounding him. This extreme sincerity inherent in his being will provide one of the concrete evidences that he is the real Jesus (as).

The Appearance of False Messiahs Foretells the Coming of Jesus (as)

True believers will recognise Jesus (as) from the portents. Every deed of his will be wise and inimitable; these portents will set him apart from other people, and he will immediately be recognised without the need for any proof. The very efforts of the false messiahs to prove themselves to be Jesus (as) will be the clearest indication that they are, in fact, imposters. Prophet Jesus' (as) actions will constitute the proof of his identity. He will inflict a terrible defeat on atheistic movements and systems that attempt to spread denial of Allah and to spread immorality. It will be easy for him to thwart the plots of the deniers with the revelation of Allah, to spread Allah's religion among people and to negate the efforts of the ungodly. By his miracles he will prove that the religion of Allah is the true way and that believers will inevitably have the upper hand. In the Qur'an Allah gives these glad tidings to believers:

> **They desire to extinguish Allah's Light with their mouths but Allah will perfect His Light, though the unbelievers hate it. It is He Who sent His Messenger with guidance and the Religion of Truth to exalt it over every other religion, though the associators hate it. (Surat as-Saff: 8-9)**

He Will Have No Relatives, Family or Acquaintances on Earth

Jesus (as) will be recognisable by these attributes mentioned in the Qur'an. However, there will be other factors disclosing his identity. One of them will be the fact that he will have no relatives, family or acquaintances on earth. There will be no one who knows his physical features, his face or the tone of his voice. Indeed, no one will know him when he comes to earth for the second time simply because the people who knew him lived and died some two thousand years ago. His mother Maryam (as), the Prophet Zakariyyah (as), the disciples who spent years at his side, prominent Jews of the time and even those people who heard Jesus' (as) revelations are all long dead. Thus, in his second coming to earth no one will have witnessed his birth, childhood, youth or adulthood. Nobody will know anything about him. As explained in earlier sections of the book, Jesus (as) came into existence by the command of Allah, the command "Be!" After two millennia, it is very natural that he will have no relatives on earth. Allah draws an analogy between his situation and that of Adam (as) when He states:

The likeness of 'Isa in Allah's sight is the same as Adam. He created him from earth and then He said to Him: "Be!" and he was. (Surah Al 'Imran: 59)

As mentioned in the verse, Allah gave the command "Be!" to Adam (as) and he was accordingly created. The way Jesus (as) came into existence for the first time also occurred in the same way although he had a mother. Adam (as) had no parents and neither will Jesus (as) at his second coming. Hundreds of years later, he will be on the earth with no known kin.

When Jesus (as) returns to earth there will be no doubt as to his true identity. The lies of those who falsely claim to be the messiah will be seen through easily. It would be impossible for someone who has spent his entire childhood amongst people and whom countless people have known ever since he was very young, to claim to be Jesus (as).

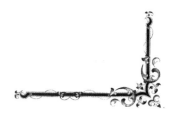

CONCLUSION

*T*hat Jesus (as) will be sent back to earth for a second time by Allah is surely a Divine favour to all humanity. Only a minority of people will enjoy this occasion. He will then be a blessed saviour sent to all mankind. Indeed, in times when violence and disorder were increasingly experienced in the world, human beings begged a helper from Allah. Accordingly, Allah responded to their plea:

> **What reason could you have for not fighting in the Way of Allah – for those men, women and children who are oppressed and say, "Our Lord, take us out of this city whose inhabitants are wrongdoers! Give us a protector from You! Give us a helper from You!"? (Surat an-Nisa: 75)**

As mentioned earlier, the saviour in our time is the penetration of the Qur'anic values to our souls and society. Upon his second coming, Jesus (as) will wholeheartedly communicate these revealed values favoured by Allah and strive purely to spread them to people all over the world.

The knowledge of unseen and future events is something only known to Allah. Yet, it is certain that those who expect this blessed period and this person must at that time undertake important obligations. Just as Jesus (as) will protect and guide all believers, the believers must also give their wholehearted support to Jesus (as) and help him in the services he renders for the sake of Allah.

Any idleness with regard to welcoming such an important guest will of course be morally unacceptable. No one, who has faith in Allah's verses, and is aware of world developments and the signs of the end times, can decide not to prepare for this blessed visitor. Those who follow the messengers of Allah, who provide them sincere support and adopt the revealed values brought by them may well hope to earn the good pleasure, mercy and eternal paradise of Allah. This is a definite promise and good tidings given by Allah:

... Allah has sent down a reminder to you, a Messenger reciting Allah's Clear Signs to you to bring those who have faith and do right actions out of the darkness into the Light. Whoever has faith in Allah and acts rightly, We will admit him into Gardens with rivers flowing under them remaining in them timelessly, for ever and ever. Allah has provided for him excellently! (Surat at-Talaq: 10-11)

They said 'Glory be to You!
We have no knowledge except what
You have taught us.
You are the All-Knowing,
the All-Wise.'
(Surat al-Baqara: 32)

NOTES

1. Reports and traditions on the sayings and actions of the Prophet Muhammad (saas)

2. The word 'Mahdi' literally means The Guided One and this will be someone who, alongside Jesus (as) will work to reform society towards Islam before the Day of Judgement.

3. Narrated by Abu Hudhayfa; Sahih Bukhari;; *Being the Tradition of Saying and Doings of the Prophet Muhammad as Narrated by His Companions*, New Delhi, Islamic Book Service, 2002, hadith no. 6324, 239; Tafsir Ibn Kathir, abridged by Sheikh Muhammad Nasib ar-Rafa'i, London, Al-Firdous Ltd., 1999, 176

4. Ibn Kathir, *Tafsir al-Qur'an al-'Azim*, 1:573-576, Cairo, 1996

5. Imam Muhammad Zahid al-Kawthari, *Nazra 'Abira fi Maza'im Man Yankur Nuzul 'Isa 'alyhi al-Salam aabla al-Akhira (A Cursory Look at the Claims of Those Who Deny Jesus' Descent before the Next Life)*, Egypt, 1980, pp. 34-37

6. Abu Mansur Muhammad al-Maturidi, *Kitab Tawilat al-Qur'an*, Beirut, p. 67

7. Ibn Jarir al-Tabari, *Tafsir al-Tabari*, 3:290-291, Beirut, 1997

8. Hamdi Yazir of Elmali, *Hak Din Kuran Dili (The True Religion, the Language of the Qur'an)*, 2:1112-1113, Eser Publishing, Istanbul, 1971

9. Al-Ash'ari, *Al-Ash'ari's al-Ibana 'an Usul al-Diyana*, Cairo, 1986, 2:115

10 Hasan Basri Cantay, *Kuran-i Hakim ve Meal-i Kerim (Tafsir of the Qur'an)*, Risale Publishing, Istanbul, 1980, 1:92

11. Imam Ibn Taymiyya, *Majmu' Fatawa*, trans. by Abdurrahman ibn Muhammad ibn Qasim al-Asimi an-Najdi, 4:323

12. Al-Kawthari, *Nazra 'Abira fi Maza'im*, p. 93

13. Sheikh al-Islam Mustafa Sabri, *Maw[...] al-'Aql (Position of Reason)*, Beirut, 1992, 233

14. Said Ramadan al-Buti, *Islam Aka[...] (Islamic Catechism)*, Istanbul, Mavde Pu[...] lishings, 1996, p. 338

15. Ömer Nasuhi Bilmen, *Kuran-i Kerim' Türkce Meali Alisi ve Tefsiri (The Turki[...] Translation of the Noble Qur'an and Its Cor[...] mentary)*, Timas Publishing, Istanbul, 8[...] edition, Volume 7, p. 3292

16. Prof. Suleyman Ates, *Yuce Kur'an' Cagdas Tefsiri (The Contemporary Tafsir of t[...] Holy Qur'an)*, Istanbul, 1988-1992, vol. 6, 4281

17. Sayyid Qutb, *Fi Zilal al-Qur'an (In t[...] Shade of the Qur'an)*, www.sevde.de/ Kuran-Tevsiri/Kuran_Tefsiri.htm

18. Imam Muhammad Zahid al-Kawtha[...] *Nazra 'Abira fi Maza'im Man Yankur Nuz[...] 'Isa 'alyhi al-Salam aabla al-Akhira (A Curs[...] ry Look at the Claims of Those Who Den[...] Jesus' Descent before the Next Life)*, Egyp[...] 1980, p. 105

19. Omer Nasuhi Bilmen, *Kuran-i Kerim'[...] Türkce Meali Alisi ve Tefsiri (The Turkis[...] Translation of the Noble Qur'an and Its Con[...] mentary)*, Timas Publishing, Istanbul, 8[...] edition, Volume 7, p. 3292

20. Muhammed Khalil Herras, *Fasl a[...] maqal fi raf'i 'Isa hayyan wa nuzulihi wa qat[...] hi'd-Dajjal (The Ascend of Jesus, His Reviv[...] Resurrection, and His Killing the Dajjal*, Makatabat as-Sunnah, Cairo, 1990, p. 20

21. Imam at-Tabari, *The Commentary of a[...] Tabari*, Vol. 1, p. 247

22. Imam Abu Hanifa, *Al-Fiqh al-Akba[...]* http://muslim-canada.org/fiqh.htm

23. Said-i Nursi, *The Letters, The Fifteent[...] Letter*, Sozler Publishing, Istanbul, 1980, [...] 54

24. Said-i Nursi, *The Rays, The Fifth Ra[...]* Sozler Publishing, Istanbul, 1980, p. 487

ALSO BY HARUN YAHYA

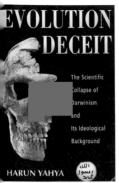

Many people think that Darwin's Theory of Evolution is a proven fact. Contrary to this conventional wisdom, recent developments in science completely disprove the theory. The only reason Darwinism is still foisted on people by means of a worldwide propaganda campaign lies in the ideological aspects of the theory. All secular ideologies and philosophies try to provide a basis for themselves by relying on the theory of evolution.

This book clarifies the scientific collapse of the theory of evolution in a way that is detailed but easy to understand. It reveals the frauds and distortions committed by evolutionists to "prove" evolution. Finally it analyzes the powers and motives that strive to keep this theory alive and make people believe in it.

Anyone who wants to learn about the origin of living things, including mankind, needs to read this book.

238 PAGES WITH 166 PICTURESIN COLOUR

One of the purposes why the Qur'an was revealed is to summon people to think about creation and its works. When a person examines his own body and any other living thing in nature, the world or the whole universe, in it he sees a great design, art, plan and intelligence. All this is evidence proving Allah's being, unit, and eternal power.

For Men of Understanding was written to make the reader see and realise some of the evidence of creation in nature. Many living miracles are revealed in the book with hundreds of pictures and brief explanations.

288 PAGES WITH 467 PICTURES IN COLOUR

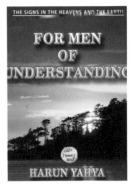

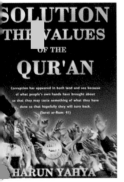

People who are oppressed, who are tortured to death, innocent babies, those who cannot afford even a loaf of bread, who must sleep in tents or even in streets in cold weather, those who are massacred just because they belong to a certain tribe, women, children, and old people who are expelled from their homes because of their religion... Eventually, there is only one solution to the injustice, chaos, terror, massacres, hunger, poverty, and oppression: the morals of the Qur'an.

208 PAGES WITH 276 PICTURES IN COLOUR

This book gives an insight into some good moral aspects of the Karma philosophy which are in agreement with the Qur'an, as well as its twisted views which conflict with human reason and conscience. The book also explains why following Allah's way and living by the Qur'an is the only way to real happiness, peace, and security.

Have you ever thought that you were non-existent before you were born and suddenly appeared on Earth? Have you ever thought that the peel of a banana, melon, watermelon or an orange each serve as a quality package preserving the fruit's odour and taste?

Man is a being to which Allah has granted the faculty of thinking. Yet a majority of people fail to employ this faculty as they should… The purpose of this book is to summon people to think in the way they should and to guide them in their efforts to think.

128 PAGES WITH 137 PICTURES IN COLOUR

Darwin said: "If it could be demonstrated that any complex organ existed, which could not possibly have been formed by numerous, successive, slight modifications, my theory would absolutely break down." When you read this book, you will see that Darwin's theory has absolutely broken down, just as he feared it would.

A thorough examination of the feathers of a bird, the sonar system of a bat or the wing structure of a fly reveal amazingly complex designs. And these designs indicate that they are created flawlessly by Allah.

208 PAGES WITH 302 PICTURES IN COLOUR

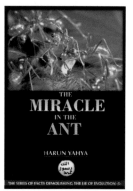

The evidence of Allah's creation is present everywhere in the universe. A person comes across many of these proofs in the course of his daily life; yet if he does not think deeply, he may wrongly consider them to be trivial details. In fact in every creature there are great mysteries to be pondered.

These millimeter-sized animals that we frequently come across but don't care much about have an excellent ability for organization and specialization that is not to be matched by any other being on earth. These aspects of ants create in one a great admiration for Allah's superior power and unmatched creation.

165 PAGES WITH 104 PICTURES IN COLOUR

Never plead ignorance of Allah's evident existence, that everything was created by Allah, that everything you own was given to you by Allah for your subsistence, that you will not stay so long in this world, of the reality of death, that the Qur'an is the Book of truth, that you will give account for your deeds, of the voice of your conscience that always invites you to righteousness, of the existence of the hereafter and the day of account, that hell is the eternal home of severe punishment, and of the reality of fate.

112 PAGES WITH 74 PICTURES IN COLOUR

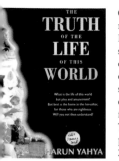

One of the major reasons why people feel a profound sense of attachment to life and cast religion aside is the assumption that life is eternal. Forgetting that death is likely to put an end to this life at any time, man simply believes that he can enjoy a perfect and happy life. Yet he evidently deceives himself. The world is a temporary place specially created by Allah to test man. That is why, it is inherently flawed and far from satisfying man's endless needs and desires. Each and every attraction existing in the world eventually wears out, becomes corrupt, decays and finally disappears. This is the never-changing reality of life.

This book explains this most important essence of life and leads man to ponder the real place to which he belongs, namely the Hereafter.

224 PAGES WITH 144 PICTURES IN COLOUR

any societies that rebelled against the will of Allah or regarded His essengers as enemies were wiped off the face of the earth completely... ll of them were destroyed–some by a volcanic eruption, some by a distrous flood, and some by a sand storm... erished Nations examines these penalties as revealed in the verses of e Quran and in light of archaeological discoveries.

9 PAGES WITH 73 PICTURES IN COLOUR

Colours, patterns, spots, even lines of each living being existing in nature have a meaning. For some species, colours serve as a communication tool; for others, they are a warning against enemies. Whatever the case, these colours are essential for the well-being of living beings. An attentive eye would immediately recognise that not only the living beings, but also everything in nature are just as they should be. Furthermore, he would realise that everything is given to the service of man: the comforting blue colour of the sky, the colourful view of flowers, the bright green trees and meadows, the moon and stars illuminating the world in pitch darkness together with innumerable beauties surrounding man…

160 PAGES WITH 215 PICTURES IN COLOUR

In a body that is made up of atoms, you breathe in air, eat food, and drink liquids that are all composed of atoms. Everything you see is nothing but the result of the collision of electrons of atoms with photons.

In this book, the implausibility of the spontaneous formation of an atom, the building-block of everything, living or non-living, is related and the flawless nature of Allah's creation is demonstrated.

139 PAGES WITH 122 PICTURES IN COLOUR

CHILDREN'S BOOKS

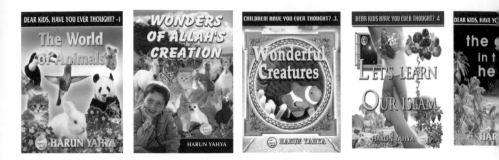

HARUN YAHYA ON THE INTERNET

YOU CAN FIND ALL THE WORKS OF HARUN YAHYA ON THE INTERNET

www.harunyahya.com
e-mail: info@harunyahya.com